A HAPPY HEART

...One man's inspiring story of God's fulfilment in his life

A HAPPY HEART
...One man's inspiring story of God's fulfilment in his life

Dr. Roy Lake Mainse

FOREWARD

by

David Mainse

CROSSROADS CHRISTIAN COMMUNICATIONS INC.
100 Huntley Street, Toronto, Ontario M4Y 2L1

Copyright 1988 ©**CROSSROADS CHRISTIAN COMMUNICATIONS INC.**

Published by **CROSSROADS CHRISTIAN COMMUNICATIONS INC.**
100 Huntley Street, Toronto, Ontario, Canada M4Y 2L1

Printed in Canada
Harmony Printing Limited
123 Eastside Drive, Toronto, Ontario, Canada M8Z 5S5

Contents

Foreward

For over two years now in our ministry we've been emphasizing "Household Salvation," winning your whole family to Jesus. I believe that by publishing and distributing this book, we'll help lift your faith more than ever to claim all your loved ones for the Lord.

As far as I know, Dad intended the manuscript just for his family. He desired "Household Salvation", and leaving his testimony behind him was for that purpose.

After Dad died in 1972, Norma-Jean and I, along with our four children, Elaine, Ellen, Reynold and Ron, read this from Dad's own handwriting twice around our family alter over a period of several months. What a blessing it was to our family!

He wrote of his wife and my mother, who died when I was only 12, "In the 24 years of our married life, I never heard her say one word out of place. She would never criticize anybody, but would always try to help everyone to her Lord."

One of my strong memories of mother is her last public testimony for Jesus before she died. She quoted Joshua, the hero of God who led Israel from the wilderness into the promised land, "But as for me and my house, we will serve the Lord." Joshua 24:15

May all who read this be blessed.

David Mainse

Introduction

Last night February 12, 1960 while lying awake, a voice said unto me, "Write an account of your life." When I arose this morning it was clearly in my mind, so here I take my pen to make a start. I don't know the purpose of that voice but if I obey it (that voice) and do my part, I am sure some glory will result to my gracious Lord and Saviour. My part is to obey and my Lord's part is to give me what He would have me write; so I commit my mind for His guidance and assistance. He gave me Psalm 121, of which I will relate later. It has been my Psalm ever since. I take it as my sufficiency in this undertaking. It has been my support and stay for nearly eight years now, and it will continue to be my support until He says, "That is enough, come up higher."

Roy L. Mainse

DR. ROY LAKE MAINSE
1896-1972

TIME

"When as a child, I laughed and wept,
Time crept;
When as a youth, I dreamed and talked,
Time walked;
When I became a full grown man,
Time ran;
When older still I daily grew,
Time flew;
Soon I shall find in travelling on,
Time gone"

Chapter One

United Empire Loyalists

When one goes to speak of his forefathers, one is a little embarrassed, and doesn't want to appear to glory in those who have passed on to their reward. Nevertheless, I feel that something should be said regarding my forebearers.

My father, Allan S. Mainse, born at Sweet's Corners, Ontario, May 25, 1863, was the son of Joseph Mainse and his wife Hester Ann Sweet. Joseph Mainse was the son of one of the engineers who engineered the building of the Rideau Canal and was lock-master at Jone's Falls for some time. His wife was the daughter of Allan Sweet, born in the U.S.A., September 10th, 1785 who came to Canada in 1811 or 1812 as a United Empire Loyalist, and settled on virgin land received from the Government. His wife, whom he had married in 1810 died shortly after his coming to Canada. On the 6th of August 1815, he took to himself a second wife, Desire Sly. From this union, there were nine children. One of these children was my Grandmother, who when she married Joseph Mainse, settled on the hundred acres of land given her by the Government. The farm is still in the Mainse family at Sweet's Corners.

My mother was Parthena Snider, daughter of Charles Snider, born September 1st 1827, who when he came out from Ireland, settled on a large tract of virgin lumber land, given him by the Government, around Mazinaw Lake, near Cloyne, Ontario. He developed the lumber business by building a dam and a saw-mill where the Mississippi River flows out of the Mazinaw. His helpers used to float squared timbers down the Mississippi River, the Ottawa River into the St. Lawrence River and on down to Quebec, where they were loaded on ships for the British Isles. Grandfather Snider claimed that he felled enough virgin pine into the Mazinaw Lake, (which pine got into a whirlpool and sank to the bottom of the lake,) to make any man independently rich, if they were to be raised. He claimed that those monstrous trees would be sound and good as the day they took their watery dive after some years. Later Grandfather sold out to a Mr. MacLaren for $10,000.00 and bought a farm near Odessa, Ontario, where he lived the remainder of his life, departing this world, October 26th, 1901.

It was at this farm near Odessa, that my father used to go to see his girlfriend, Miss P. Snider. One time when he had driven the forty odd miles to see her, she told him that she had been converted in Salvation Army meetings, and had given her heart to the Lord. As a result of her conversion, she had put off her finery and was dressed very plainly. Father was greatly upset by the change in her appearance, and told her that if she were going to go that way that he was through with her. Miss Snider let him know that this was the way she was going, so her suitor went away in a rage. After he drove a little distance, he began to cool down, then he asked himself, "Well, what kind of a wife do I want? Don't I want a Christian like my Mother?" He decided on the road between Odessa and Kingston that he wanted a Christian wife. He turned around, went back to the Snider home and asked Miss Snider to forgive him, which she freely did. Not long after, on the 17th day of October, 1888, they were happily united in marriage. To this union, ten children were born, three having predeceased them in their childhood, and seven of us are still living. The oldest of us, and only daughter living is Mrs. D. Ford Kenny, the mother of three missionaries, two of them to Egypt, and one, Roy to Brazil, and there are six other children,

Charles, myself, Stuart, Ernest, Ross and Edward.

I, Roy Lake Mainse, am the third living one in this family of seven. I was born November 30th, 1896, at Sweet's Corners, Ontario.

Chapter Two

"Home"

After Allan S. Mainse and Parthena Snider were united in holy matrimony, they bought Grandmother Mainse's sister's farm that she had received also from the Government. It was right next to the Mainse Homestead. Father's brother, Edward F. Mainse, remained on the homestead, so side by side, they lived and worked harmoniously together. Both of them were christian men, and for years they had only one purse and never a word of complaint from either one. It was only after some years, that they decided it would be better to have two purses instead of one, so they very agreeably divided all assets, but continued to work together as a team, until we boys were large enough to help each of our parents.

An incident that greatly influenced my childhood and teen life happened to my older brother, Charles, when he was four years old. Father had taken the wooden pump out of the stoned-up well at the barn to have repairs made on it. He had covered the fourteen inch square hole with a board, and started off to the village with the pump. Charlie, as a boy, with an inquisitive bump, thought he would like to see what was in that covered up hole. He removed the board, stuck his head down to see, and in he went, head first. Mother missed her lad, and went to the kitchen door to see where he was. She saw him and he was crawling on his hands and knees, coming out of the horse stables. Oh, she thought, he has been kicked by a horse. She ran to get him and found him soaking wet; and so cold that he couldn't speak. She ran with him to the house, ran out to the road and called Uncle Edward Mainse, who came running up. When he saw Charlie's condition, he hitched up a horse, hastened to the village for father and the family doctor. While he was gone Mother got a fire in the stove, changed Charlie's wet clothes, and wrapped him in woolen blankets. By the time Uncle and father got back with the Doctor, Charlie was getting so he could speak.

The Doctor asked Charlie, "Well son, what happened to you?" With his teeth still chattering, he said, "I fell in the well." Doctor said, "And how did you get out?" "Well", he said, "I tried to climb up, and I would fall back in again. I saw I was going to die, and I just asked the Lord to help me out, and He came down, put His arms underneath me, and set me on the top." Dr. Cregan scratched his head, looked at Father, and said, "I want to see that well." Down they went to the well. The Doctor asked Father if he would go down the well, measure the depth to the water and the water in the well. Father went down stretching his legs from side to side, finding places for his feet in the stones. It was sixteen feet to the water, and six feet of water in the well, and Charlie's little straw hat he fished out of the bottom of the well.

When Father came up the Doctor stood there nodding his head and saying, "That is a miracle." Oh, how often I have heard Father and Mother tell of that happening while I was a boy and even in my teens, and I delighted to hear them tell it. It always did something to me to hear it told, and it does still whenever I tell it today. Surely, "God works in a mysterious way, His wonders to perform."

My Father and Mother were very devoted to the Lord and His cause. Father went out preaching on a circuit for two to three years, then gave up the circuit work for local preaching. He held a number of revivals locally in which a number of people were saved and added to the church. Truly, he was a power in prayer, and could pray souls through to victory.

As a boy five years old, I was converted in some children's meetings that my father held in our home for us and the neighbouring children. It truly was wonderful to be saved. I was very happy for some time, then I felt the Lord wanted me to go and pray with some neighbour children; but I felt that I was too young and small to do such a thing; so I failed to go and gave up praying and testifying. I didn't go into outward sin, even for years, but I was a sinner nevertheless.

When I was in my middle teens, there was a dance held in the Orange Hall a mile and a half from my home, I decided that I was going to it. Father was away, so I thought it a good chance to go. I went upstairs, dressed up, and as I came down to go to the dance, my Father came walking into the house. He asked, "Where are you going, Roy?" I replied, "I'm going up to the Orange Hall." Very authoritively, he said, "No, you are not.", and that was all he said. I went back upstairs, felt badly for a while, then, I began to think that he knows better than I do about dances, so it must be better for me not to go to dances. Then I was rather glad that Father came home when he did. Never again was I tempted to go to a dance. I happened to get into one at a Red Cross Meeting. When the business of the meeting was done, and the eats were taken care of, the folk began to clear the floor for a dance. I waited around 'til they started to dance, and was I ever disgusted with the foolishness of it all. I immediately got my coat and hat, and left them to their folly, and went contentedly homeward.

The Spirit of God continued to talk to me. He surely was married to this poor boy backslider. I might say, that when I was around seventeen years of age, I said to the Spirit, as He strove with me, "Lord, if you will leave me alone, til' I'm twenty-one, then I will give you my heart and live for You!"

Then, at twenty-one, the Lord spoke very clearly to me and said, "You promised if I would leave you alone til' you were twenty-one, you would seek me and serve me." I said, "Yes, Lord, I did, and the first chance I get, I will seek thee."

After that conversation with the Lord, I began to pray at night by my bedside for the Lord to send such conviction on me that I would get saved. I didn't pray that prayer very long, until I had more conviction for my sins than I could handle. I would go to the weekly prayer meetings and get back in a corner of the room, where the meetings were being held; and while the people were on their knees praying, I would weep, what felt to me, scalding tears. Ere the praying was finished, I would wipe all tears away, so nobody would know that I had been weeping.

As a boy going to Public School I loved sports, especially baseball and hockey. As I grew older, the love of those games grew greater. Father used to say to me that I would rather play baseball than eat any day. He was quite right in that, indeed.

In my middle teens I was taken into the Sweet's Corners Baseball and Hockey Teams, so I considered I was doing something worthwhile. In the Baseball Team, I was appointed by our Captain as Catcher. As long as I had the mask, pad and catcher's glove on, I was no more afraid of a hard ball than I was of a soft rag ball.

At a picnic of the Methodist Church, Sweet's Corners was playing against Seeley's Bay, a village six miles from home, I was at the bat, the ball was thrown, I hit it squarely, and knocked it into the outfield. I was easily making a home run, but as I was running in from third base, the Seeley's Bay catcher jumped into me to try to hinder my touching the base. I touched the base alright, but then, I was into that catcher for a fight, but the Methodist Minister, a lame man, ran in between us and stopped us.

In that same game, I had happen the only accident that ever happened to me playing baseball. I had given the signal to the pitcher for the kind of ball I wanted him to throw, but he threw another kind of curve swiftly, and it caught me right on the end of the third finger of my right hand. It tore the nail right off, and broke the first joint. I pulled the mask, pad, and mitt off, and my older brother was then asked to be catcher. He wasn't used to catching and wasn't doing as I thought he should, so I said, "Here, give me them back again." I went ahead and played the rest of the game and we won, too. In those days, we very seldom ever bothered with a doctor for such things. I never even had a bandage on my finger, and I said nothing to my Father. If I had told him, he would have said, so I thought, "Well, that's what you get from playing baseball." So, as the saying is, I grinned and bore it, and bear I did, in my third finger, the marks of a broken finger. It is something to remind me of my love for baseball. By the way, when I got saved, I had to choose between playing on that baseball team and serving the Lord. The Captain came to me as spring opened up, and said to me, "How about playing baseball this year, Roy?" "Well," I said, "Well, I haven't thought much about it, but I will let you know in a couple of days." I asked the Lord about it, and it came to me like this – Can you associate with lads that curse and swear and break my Holy Day by practising baseball? It was temptation but not a very great one by any means, so I told the Captain that I would not be playing anymore. I had no idea that my decision would break up the baseball team, but I was their catcher and one of the best batters, so the team was never organized again.

The last game of hockey that I played was two or three nights before I was converted. It was indeed a rough game, and I was in a fighting mood. I always played left wing in the forward line, and it was just too bad for anybody that body-checked me that night, for they went down. My two hundred pounds was too much for them. The game was between Sweet's Corners and Lyndhurst. We won five to three; after that game was over, one of my good friends who played for Lyndhurst wouldn't speak to me. I had no hard feelings against him, even though I had sent him flying when he body-checked me, but he seemingly held something against me. I decided when I began seeking the Lord, that, as a Christian, I could have nothing further to do with such a rough game, that would cause hard feelings to my friends.

Chapter Three

"You Are My Child"

During this period, when God sent conviction for my sins upon me, my first cousin, Clarence Mainse, with whom I had played and frolicked as a boy, was killed in the First World War. A memorial service was held for him in the church by the pastor, Rev. J.E. Wilson. During that service, a letter was read from Clarence that he had sent his parents when he joined the Armed Forces out in Western Canada, where he was teaching school. In that letter, he told about his decision to join the Armed Forces of his Country, and he said that he had asked God to forgive him of his sins and wanted his Mother and Father to forgive him too. That confession simply broke my heart, and I promised God again that the first chance I had, I would seek Him. I could have been saved right there, but I thought I had to be at a penitent form in a Church to get saved.

During the month of January, Rev. Wilson, with the help of Rev. W.J. Thompkins, an evangelist, started revival services in the home church. I wanted to get saved, and many were attending the services even though the weather was bad. The revival services were to wind up with a three-day convention and a convention in those days always brought a great crowd around.

On Monday night, preceeding the Convention, I went to the service and sat second in the seat from the aisle. On the outside sat one of the most wicked men of our community. I seemingly was afraid to pass out of the seat in front of him. He whispered to me, "Roy, don't let me hinder your going." I very gingerly replied, "You are not hindering me." In reality, he was the very cause of my not going to the penitent form that night. I didn't go back again until Friday night of the Convention. Conviction wasn't nearly as heavy that night as on the previous Monday night. I was alarmed, and asked myself the question, "Is it possible the Holy Spirit is leaving me?" My Father came and spoke to me about seeking the Lord. While he was speaking to me, the pastor came too, and by God's help, I made for the altar. As I confessed silently to the Lord, the fountain of my heart was broken up indeed. The Lord asked me to pray out loud. I seemingly couldn't get my mouth open to say a word, so that service closed and I had no victory as yet, but I was determined to find the Lord if it took three weeks to find Him, as it did with my Father.

MY SALVATION

On Saturday morning, January 25th, 1918, I couldn't get to the church soon enough. I wanted to get back to that altar, and to it I went as soon as the call was given. Still I couldn't get my mouth open to utter a word. The afternoon service was a repetition of the morning service, except that the minister called for a testimony meeting. A number testified under the inspiration of the Holy Spirit. While Mrs. Herb Frayn was testifying, she quoted, St. Luke 11:11-13, "If a son shall ask bread of any of you that is a father, will he give him a stone. Or if he shall ask an egg, will he offer him a scorpion? If ye then being evil, know how to give good gifts unto your children: how much more shall your heavenly Father give the Holy Spirit to them that ask?" The scripture greatly inspired my faith. Then the Lord said to me, "Will you get up and tell your determination?." "Well," I thought , "I can get my mouth open to that." I arose when Mrs. Frayan sat down, and said, "I am determined to seek the Lord until I find Him." At that, my mouth literally flew open and

19

I, quite loudly indeed, was shouting the praises of my wonderful Lord. God had very graciously saved my soul from sin and its damnable degradation. How happy I was! Words could not begin to tell of the joy of the Lord that flooded my soul. Everything seemed different. We stayed in the church until after the night's service. When I went outside around 10 o'clock to go home, the stars attracted my attention. To me, they seemed to be praising the Lord, too. I couldn't help but remark that the stars were more beautiful than I had ever seen them before.

It had been announced that the Sunday morning service was to be a sacramental service, in which the emblems of the broken body and spilt blood of Jesus were distributed. As we were doing the morning chores a voice said to me, "You should not take the sacrament as you are just newly saved." "Well," I thought, "Maybe I had better not." Then that sweet voice of Jesus said, "You have a perfect right to take the sacrament. You are My Child." At that, I recognized the difference in those voices, and I said, "Yes Lord, I will take the sacrament."

A sacramental message was preached, but oh, how unworthy I felt myself; yet God had spoken and told me that I was His Child; so I bowed with the rest at the altar to partake of the emblems of His broken body and spilt blood. As soon as I had partaken, I don't know whether I was in the body or out of it; I went up to the Gate of Heaven, which opened before me and I entered therein. As I was simply sailing down a beautiful avenue that lay before me, I saw coming towards me, a company of redeemed, not walking, but floating along as I was. When we were some twenty to thirty feet apart, they all turned and looked to their right. I turned and looked to my left. Oh, the rapture of the moment! There stood Jesus with uplifted hands in blessing us. We all fell on our faces before Him praising and worshipping Him.

The people were all arising as I came to myself, so

I arose and went to my seat. Everything around seemed drab and dead after the beauty and whiteness of the celestial city. For days after, I could see before my eyes the glorious whiteness and beauty of the Saviour's countenance, the robes and garments of the redeemed saints. Once, as I was supposed to be working, my Father asked me, "What are you gazing at?" I unashamedly explained "Oh, I can still see the whiteness of that heavenly scene." Truly, it was transporting.

The devil wasn't through yet. As I was hitching up a team of colts to the light set of bob-sleighs to take a load to service, one of the colts threw its head around as I was putting up the neck-yoke, and hit me a terrific blow on the side of my head. I raised my arm to teach that colt some manners, but I caught myself just in time. Instead of delivering a mightly blow to that colt, I sent up a cry to heaven, "Oh God, help me, I'm afraid of this thing within me. Take it out of me, Lord." From that moment, I was a seeker after the death of that old man sin. My nature fairly groaned for the destruction of that monster which had so nearly over-thrown me.

My cry to God was, "Cleanse Thou, my heart." Seemingly, nearly every waking breath was a cry to God. That continued for four days. The revival meetings didn't close and I was seeking God for His holiness every night at the service as well as praying at my work all the day. On Tuesday night, there was a testimony meeting after the service. A brother was telling how he had been sanctified by the power of the Holy Spirit, and as he witnessed to the experience, my faith made contact, and a voice said to me so clearly, "You are sanctified wholly," The power of the Holy Spirit simply surged through me, wave after wave. I felt that sparks of fire were coming out of the ends of my fingers as I shook hands with the saints before the service was dismissed.

My Father always wanted me to stay on the farm with him. However in March, I believe it was, a call up of soldiers for the Army took place, and I received my notice to appear in Kingston, so I signed up, although I just felt that I couldn't use a gun to shoot anyone. I asked if I could get into the medical corp. I was told that I couldn't get into it anyway. Father went to see the General concerned. He admitted him to his office, but told Father very gruffly that he could do nothing in that line for me. Father went home that evening, not to sleep, but pray. He spent the night in prayer. I was just resting in the Lord that my God would work this matter out for me. I didn't know how, but I knew He would not fail me.

The very next morning, after Father's night of prayer, the phone rang, calling long distance from Kingston, wanting Allan Mainse, and Father answered. On the other end of the line, he heard, "This is General So and So. I have changed my mind regarding your son Roy Mainse. I am putting him in special service here in Canada." Father thanked him and the conversation was over. Shortly after the conversation, father was on his way to Kingston to tell me that I was being transferred to another unit of the Army. God still answers prayer. Praise His Name! With God, all things are possible.

That day or the next, I am not just certain which, I was taken to old Fort Henry and did guard duty some of the time, did office work in the Colonel's Office, and had a clear conscience before God. Many a time, I would go out back of Old Fort Henry and pray the blessing of heaven down upon my soul, and go back into the Fort more than a conquerer.

Once during the summer of 1918 the whole heavens became very red and dangerous looking. Many of the soldiers were frightened and began to pray, and to dig down into their kit-bags and get their Testaments out and read them. I heard them say one to the other. "My, I wish I was like Mainse, he is not afraid at all." But when it passed over, which was in an hour or two, they forgot all about it, and went on their apparently unchanged way. Nevertheless, I must say, that the soldiers in our room were very respectful when I would be reading my Bible and kneeling beside my bed in prayer.

One day in the month of December, 1918, after the war was over, I was in the Colonel's Office doing some work, when he called me to his desk. I saluted, then he said, "I want you to take this," handing me a sealed envelope, "to a certain army office down in the city, and bring back the parcel they give you." I saluted again, and told him that I would immediately do so. After an hour or a little more, I was back, saluted, and gave him the little parcel. He took it, opened it, took out an honourable service pin, and pinned it on my tunic. I thanked him profusely, and went on with my duties. I was told by the other soldiers that I was the only one in Fort Henry who received an honourable service pin.

Around the middle of January 1919, I received my discharge from the Army, and went home to take up my duties on the farm once again.

Chapter Four

"Preach or be Damned"

During the spring and summer of 1919, I felt a special urge that I should enter the work of the Lord. I would tell the Lord that I would go, and then I would put it off, only to find a spiritual dryness developing deep within. I really didn't want to preach. I wanted to farm. We had everything just right with which to farm our three farms, and I was in the business of raising pigs besides; so, all in all, I was quite engrossed with what I was doing, but the Lord was calling me to leave all and follow Him.

Rev. Peter Wiseman had been appointed Principal of Annesley College during that summer, and he approached me at our district camp meeting and asked me, "Do you not feel God is calling you to the work of the Lord?" I wouldn't admit whether He was or He wasn't calling. Then my aunt, Mrs. Philip Robeson, who lived near Athens, Ontario, broached the subject that same fall. She said, "Roy, I feel God is calling you to preach the gospel. You want to obey the Lord's call, etc." I wanted to do the will of the Lord, but I wanted even more for the Lord's will to be what I wanted.

About the tenth of January, 1920, the Kingston Ontario Holiness Movement Church was holding a three-day convention, so I decided that I would go Saturday morning and come back home Monday morning. I knew that God's hand was upon me to preach, but I was holding back. During the altar service Sunday morning, the Lord headed things right up. He said to me so clearly and definitely, "Will you preach, or be damned?" It didn't take me a second to make my decision when it was put that way. I cried out, "Lord, I will preach!" Then all heaven seemed to fall into my soul. It was settled once and forever what the will of the Lord was for me. Never for one moment since that day have I looked back to the purebred Holstein cattle, or the pigs, or the farms, to hanker after them.

On Monday morning, as planned, I went home from the convention, told Father and Mother that the Lord had called me to preach the gospel, and that I was leaving for Annesley College in Ottawa as soon as possible. They didn't congratulate me; they appeared rather sad, as Father had set his heart on having me at home with him on the farm. He never said one word to discourage me or to hinder my going, but he never said a word to encourage or help me either. Once, early in the three years I spent in Annesley College, he gave me a five or ten dollar bill, I don't know which it was, and I never once said one word about money to him.

My father, some two or three years before, had asked me to lend a certain party two hundred dollars. Because it was my father who asked me, I lent it, receiving a promissory note from that party. That was all that I ever received for that two hundred dollars, and that is forty-five years ago. But the Lord had been with me during those teen years, and I had saved and I had in the bank eleven hundred dollars when God called me to preach.

Chapter Five

College Days

On the Wednesday morning, two days after coming home from the convention, I took the train from Forfar, Ontario, and two or three hours later I arrived at Ottawa. I left my trunk at the station for the time-being, boarded the street car, and walked in on Brother Peter Wiseman at Annesley College. I was given a very hearty welcome by the Wiseman's and I settled right into the studious life without the least difficulty.

After completing my first year, I was sent to work for the Lord in Montreal, Quebec. I visited, preached and studied the whole summer, and then left for Annesley again on the first of September.

Our Church Conference was also held during the early fall. Bishop Warren asked me if I would consider joining the conference.

I had around a dozen theological studies finished. That was sufficient to join the conference. I was duly called before the conference which convened in the Fifth Avenue Church in Ottawa. They asked me if I would step outside the auditorium while they discussed my application. Someone called me back in, but I guess it was a bit too early, as that dear man, Rev. T.D. Roe, was still speaking or was almost finished. I heard him speaking words that encouraged me very much. He said, " . . . a good name is rather to be chosen than great riches." He loved me and I surely did love him. From what I heard of his speech, I had something to strive for, even a good name. The good name that I have to live up to is, "Christian." I trust the Lord has helped me to do so all of these years.

That fall, I started the final group of high school subjects, along with three or four more theological studies. By dint of much hard work I got through the year very nicely, passed my high school subjects, and the theological exams were written successfully.

Of course, I spent occasional weekends in Alcove, Quebec, taking the services and seeing a very special lady friend, Miss Hazel Pritchard, whom I had met in Ottawa. Hazel travelled every week to study music at the Ottawa Conservatory and also to give music lessons to some pupils in the city. Some three years later and thousands of miles away, we would be joined, til death do us part.

In the latter part of May, the church's Annual Feast of Pentecost was held at Stittsville, Ontario. Because of a cold spell, we met in the church rather than on the camp grounds. One service of that Feast stands out in my memory. Bishop Warren was preaching, and as he preached, the Holy Spirit simply enveloped him. It is unexplainable, that is all that I can say about it. He, the Holy Spirit, simply came upon me again in mightier power than ever before. This time, I saw a crowd of people before me that I did not recognize, and I was to reach them for God.

At that Feast, when the preacher's stationing list was read out, I was stationed at Stittsville, the very place where we were meeting. I needed a horse and buggy to get around and as I went home for a few days before taking this new responsibility, my father very kindly said, "Roy you can have Skip (a beautiful driver) and my best buggy for the summer." So Father gave me help that summer in transportation, and even though it wasn't in cash, I appreciated it very much.

When the summer finished, I returned Skip to my home and I started back for Annesley. It was another good year, with more theological subjects written off, and another year of high school work done. The plan was, that another year would finish high school work and give me matriculation. Just as we began the year, conference time came around again. I had been in the college, preached regularly on Sundays, and often at that special place, Alcove, Quebec. As a result, the conference agreed to the report brought in by the committee on Orders, that I should be ordained Deacon, which was duly carried out by Bishop Warren. Truly, it was a time of very special blessing. I will never forget it as long as I live. It is vivid in my memory still.

When that school year was almost over, the Feast of Pentecost came around again. We were given a few days off from college to attend the Feast, and it was a feast to us. During the Feast, the Missionary Board met and couldn't get anyone to answer the call of Rev. J.C. Black for help in Egypt. A number had been asked if they would consider going to Egypt, but each had given a negative answer. Bishop Warren was quite exercised about it. On Saturday night, before retiring on the Stittsville camp grounds, he had asked someone to take the Sunday morning service. After retiring, he said that the Lord began talking to him and then gave him a text, and told him that He wanted him to preach in the morning. So he had to get up, dress and hunt up the Brother whom he had asked to preach, and tell him that he had been told by the Lord that he was to take the Sunday morning service himself.

Chapter Six

"I Want You to go to Egypt"

Sunday morning dawned clear and warm and by service time, the tabernacle was almost filled. The service progressed as usual. Bishop Warren gave his text, "Lift up your eyes, and look on the fields, for they are white already to harvest." He preached a great sermon and as he was about finished, the Lord of the Harvest said to me more distinctly than if Bishop Warren had said it, "I want you to go to Egypt." I could sit still no longer. I jumped to my feet and told what the Lord had said to me. Weeping and praising the Lord were the sounds that were heard all over that large tabernacle. It was truly a time when "Heaven came down our souls to greet, and glory crowned the Mercy Seat." Brother Warren said, "What we couldn't do, the Lord has done." At that time, of course, I knew nothing about the difficulty that the Missionary Board was having in finding someone to go to Egypt. The Board met again shortly and wanted me to go to Egypt in the fall. I felt that I should finish high school, so they suggested that I stay in Annesley College, study all summer and in September, write my matriculation exams at the time of the supplementary exams for all students.

When Brother Clifford Trimble, my classmate through the years, heard of my decision, he decided that he would like to do the same, so he, his wife and baby kept house in Annesley College, and I boarded with them. Clifford and I studied days and much of the night all summer and wrote our matriculation exams in September. At the conference that fall, having also completed the theological subjects, I was recommended to Elders Orders, and was ordained an Elder of the Church of Jesus Christ. God set His sanction upon it in my own heart again in a very wonderful way.

Reverend J.W. Campbell, the Missionary Board's secretary treasurer, purchased the ticket for me on the "City Line." However, I had to wait until just after Christmas for a boat on that line. It was to sail at the end of December, but when I got to New York, the Company officials said that it would still be three or four days yet before it would sail. It was only a seven thousand ton ship and was the Atlantic Ocean ever rough. That "City of Benares" tossed about like a cork, but thank the Lord, I was not sick. I even enjoyed the rolling and the tossing of the ship. There were a number of missionaries on board. Some were going to different points in Africa, while others were going to India.

One Sunday, I was chosen by the missionaries to conduct the Sunday night service in the first-class dining saloon. Oh, it was very windy, and the boat was rolling so much that I could not stand without support to preach. There was a pillar near where I was to stand, so I got one arm around it, held my Bible with the other hand, and in such a fashion I delivered part of my message, then I sat down and finished the rest of it.

One of the missionaries of the Quaker Denomination, Mr. Gilson, was going back to the Congo for his third term. He told me a couple of stories of his original team of four young men who went to open up work inland, some considerable distance from the east coast of Africa. If these stories influence you as they have me, they will be well worth telling and you will never forget them.

When Mr. Gilson and his companions arrived at the port of disembarkation, they unloaded their luggage, which consisted of seventy boxes. These they stood some place, and went light handed inland to find a place to set up their mission station. After some days' travel, they came to a tribe that very much interested them, so they decided to make that tribe of people the natives with which they would work. Here they set up their station. While there, three of the young men fell sick of malaria fever, and they had no quinine left. Mr. Gilson escaped the fever, so it was decided that he should take seventy men offered by the Chief of the tribe, go to the coast, and bring to the village the seventy boxes, which contained their medicines.

Before he left with the seventy men, the Chief pointed out a mountain to him and said, "Be sure and not stop on that mountain over night, for there are man-eaters in that mountain. If you pass over it during the daytime, you are all right, but at night, they will kill you and eat you." Everything went well until they were returning and they approached the mountain. They would have been all right but some of his men for no known reason, threw down their boxes and ran off. That delayed them for they had to carry the boxes in relays, as one box was all that a man could carry. It meant that they were climbing the mountain as the sun was receding in the west. When they got to the top, the sun was just setting, and as they looked around, they could spy some cannibals hiding in the trees. His men became so frightened that they threw down their boxes and ran for their lives. This left Mr. Gilson alone with his seventy precious boxes.

Mr. Gilson said, "What could I do? I could not leave my boxes, and there I could see those cannibals in the trees with their white teeth showing, ready to pounce upon me." "Well," he said, "I piled up those seventy boxes, climbed on top of them, got on my knees, and began to pray as I had never prayed before in all my life. God came down in such power that I was jumping up and down on the top of those boxes, shouting the praises of God. All at once, I heard some people shouting at the top of their voices. I looked and there was a large group of men running towards me from another mountain. It wasn't long before they were all around me, talking and pointing to the trees. The head man gave an order, and men picked up my seventy boxes and marched off, myself with them. They carried those boxes right to the tribe where I wanted to go."

Does God not answer prayer? As I write, my tears flow and praises spontaneously come from my lips. Our God is the God of the impossible. Praise His Holy Name!

The second story was concerning a tribe next to their tribe. A deputation came to them one day, wanting one of the missionaries to go with them, so he went. When they arrived at their village, the men said to him, "We worship a great serpent, and it comes every few days to our village, takes a child, a sheep or a goat and carries it off and eats it. We want you to shoot it with your rifle." Mr. Gilson replied, "Do you really want me to kill your god?" They answered "We don't like our god any more. We want you to kill it." He said, "Where is this great serpent?" They took him to a cliff overlooking a river; at the bottom of this cliff was a cave in which the serpent lived. It was lying asleep in the sun, stretched out on a flat rock in front of the cave. There Mr. Gilson stood with all the black men behind him looking in great fear at their god.

After looking a moment or two, Mr. Gilson raised his rifle, took aim, and fired, and the serpent began its dying contortions. The men turned and ran as fast as they could, crying at the top of their voices, "The white man has killed our god, the white man has killed our god!" So crying, they ran all of the way back to the village. When the serpent was dead, the missionary went back to the village also. The men gathered around him. He asked them, "Why did you act as you have done and cry out, 'The white man has killed our god'?" "Well," they said, "We wanted to deceive our god, and when its spirit was leaving that body, we wanted to put all of the blame on you, so that its spirit would not come back and plague us."

After that episode, Mr. Gilson told them about Jesus, who was a loving Father, as well as God, and eventually

Roy Mainse's parents, about to leave the farm to attend a funeral.

Roy L. Mainse — 1918.

Studying in front of the home farm house during a break from college.

Sometimes the quarters of Bro. Missionary and Bro. Goat
were very close by.

This travel was luxury; it generally was by donkey or foot.
Rev. Black on right.

Dad with his Egyptian brothers, Rev. Fahme, Dad's best Arabic interpreter sits to his left. It was a special thrill for me to preach in Egypt in 1968, with this same interpreter doing the honours for me.

Dad in second row and Rev. Black at the back in a conference with Egyptian Pastors.

Norma Hazel Pritchard in her beloved Gatineau Hills before travelling to Egypt and becoming Mrs. R.L. Mainse.

First Marriage, a legal one by the British Consul in Cairo.

They didn't consider themselves really married until they travelled approx. 300 miles farther south, where a fellow missionary performed the rights.

Jordan river, a honeymoon dip, 1924 style.

Rev. and Mrs. Roy L. Mainse, November 17, 1924, Cairo.

I wonder how much he will tip at the entrance to Lazarus' tomb.

Willa, Elaine and I left at home with mother for 6½ years. The missionary allowance for the family was $20.00 per month. A good garden was important.

"Here in this very spot you left me, here I am when you come back," said mother. This picture was taken just before Dad left, I was just two years old. Willa and Elaine, 10 and 8.

Mother gone now. It's important to carry on the Lord's work she loved so well.

Our final return from Egypt. I was 17 and back home to take my grade 13.

Dad re-married and takes as his help-mate Elva Bishop, a tireless worker for the cause of missions.

1958, Dad and Elva, after returning to Canada following his illness.

Here are some recent pictures of . . .

My sister Willa Hodgins

My sister Elaine Boudinot

My step-mother Elva Mainse

that tribe turned to Christ and became lowly and humble followers of the Saviour.

What a different God they had henceforth! Should we not go forth and tell to all the wonders of our God! The command is "Go ye forth into all the world, and preach the Gospel to every creature." Thank God for the privilege of going. I would go again if I were physically able. I would indeed! If you are able, won't you go? If God calls you, He will send you, and He will also meet your needs.

Eventually, our ocean liner drew near to Alexandria, Egypt, so that I could see the city in the distance. My heart yearned over those people. My burden was so great that I went down to my berth, got on my knees and consecrated myself afresh to the Lord for Egypt. It was to be my field of labour from January 1923, until March 1953 with three furloughs to Canada during that time.

As we drew into the quay, my eyes spotted that consecrated man, with whom I had come to labour, Rev. J. C. Black. He looked the same as he had when he had gone to Egypt two years before, except that his eyes looked different. The ever-shining sun of Egypt must have faded them. The sight of a fellow missionary in the crowd that thronged the quay gladdened my heart, and the excitement of the challenge gripped me again.

Before long, passport examinations were finished and I was in the land to which God had called me, the land of the Pharaohs.

Chapter Seven

"What More Could One Want?"

Egypt and its teeming multitudes were everywhere it seemed, and no matter where you went, you would hear that new language, and hardly understand a word. The very country was entirely different from Canada. People with different ways, dress, and customs. Different trees – no more maples and pines, but the fronded palms were everywhere – in field, in gardens, and even in houses with trunks growing right through the rooms, their spreading branches reaching out above the roofs. Cows tethered out in the fields stretched their necks for the grass or clover beyond their reach. Oxen yoked to an ancient plow rooted up the ground. Water buffalo lazed in the canals, with only their noses protruding out of the water. Sheep and goats were being led by the shepherds to and from the fields, where they are tethered all day long.

On our way up the Nile River, we stopped in Cairo, that great and ancient city. The great pyramid is an amazing structure. How could those great stones have been placed so high? They are four hundred and eighty feet high on a base that covers twelve acres. I don't doubt that is it called one of the wonders of the world. Beside the great pyramid, there is the famous sphynx carved out of the rock. It has a human face and a lion's great long body – seventy two feet, six inches long, and fifty-six feet high.

Travelling southward another 300 miles by train brought us into Assiut, in Central Egypt. This is where our Mission home is located. After disembarking from our coach, a carriage rumbled up through the streets into the old part of the city, which is known as "Kim Abbas", where I was to make my home. There, Rev. Black's wife, their daughter Una, and six lady missionaries gave a very warm welcome. No wonder another man was needed when there were so many fine and single ladies.

My first Sunday in Assiut, I preached through an interpreter to an Egyptian congregation. It was quite an experience. The Mission's Secretary, Mr. Sultan Butros, was given the job of teaching me Arabic. I had to apply myself to learning Arabic and getting acclimatized, along with visiting the towns and villages each weekend, where I would preach two or three times.

My second weekend in Egypt, the pastor of the church in Tahta wanted me to visit his congregation. Miss Elma Brown, one of our Missionary school teachers, was working there. I was invited to the home where she was staying for Sunday dinner. The foods were all new to me, and I was depending on Miss Brown to give leadership in what I should eat. She asked me if I would have some of a green, sloppy, soupy material. I very inappropriately said, 'I never drink tea." It was one of their main foods called "Mulakeya." They had a great laugh at my expense. I laughed too, so it passed off all right.

While there the two nights, I slept for the first time in a bed belonging to one of the village brethren. I didn't know what to expect, but I was surely expecting something, so I stayed awake practically the whole night rolling, tossing and scratching, but I couldn't see the things that I was expecting. Of course, fleas are sometimes difficult to see, and harder to catch, especially for a greenhorn at the business. I assure you, I was very green and gullible as far as the plagues of Egypt were concerned. Before many weeks and months rolled past, I was an old timer at that business. I had many a bloody battle with bed bugs and fleas, but I always had the victory, and never was I chased from the field once. The worst of it is, they are like the devil, and don't know when they are reasonably defeated. To be sure, I was not sorry when I arrived back at our Assiut headquarters, had a bath, and could study more Arabic so that I could talk to those night prowlers. They didn't seem to understand English – not even the simplest words.

Letters passed back and forth between Egypt and Canada, and in particular to the young lady from the Gatineau hills of Quebec. As a result, in the fall of 1924, Miss Norma Hazel Pritchard came to Egypt to become my bride. Rev. Black went with me to Port Said on the Mediterranean Sea to meet the bride-to-be.

I managed to get to the ship before it docked by means of a small boat, and what a happy reunion for Hazel and I, as we hadn't seen each other for two years. We travelled to Cairo, well chaperoned, where the civil ceremony took place at the British Consul at 12:00 noon. In the afternoon, we all went out to see the pyramids and sphynx, those magnificent symbols of Egypt. We didn't consider ourselves yet married, and that evening November 17, we boarded the train for Assiut, spending the entire night on the train and arriving at Assiut at 4:30 a.m.

On November 18, at 6 o'clock, Rev. J.C. Black performed the christian ceremony in the Assiut Church under an archway made of palm branches, thickly inter-woven with roses which had been made for us by a missionary friend, Miss B. Roe. Now we were really married by the Lord after the second ceremony.

Mrs. Black had prepared a great supper and a number of the Presbyterian missionaries were invited, as well as all of our own missionaries. We had a beautiful wedding and wedding supper. We missed our families, but the presence of Christ was most real, even in the centre of Egypt.

The Mission home was headquarters to all of the missionaries. Each family or single person had a large room, a common sitting room, and when we were home, we all ate together. It was fine as far as the men were concerned, but not so grand for the married ladies. It was wonderful how well Hazel and the others got along together. Yet the ladies often wished they had apartments of their own. Some few years later, in the new Mission home, apartments were supplied.

For our marriage and honeymoon, I took some time off from the evangelistic work in which I was engaged, but soon I was back at it full time again. It meant that my bride was left behind in the Mission home, but she was busy studying Arabic and visiting the homes of the women with Miss Iffa as her interpreter. Every home she visited, she preached for some fifteen minutes to the women who gathered in and then had prayers with them. Occasionally, when she would come for a weekend to the place where I was in evangelistic services, she would preach on Sunday afternoon for me. It was most acceptable too, and souls would seek the Lord as a result.

In one campaign, which was held in the village of Jowley for over three Sundays, Mrs. Mainse came to spend the last weekend with me. It was a very poor place in which I stayed – just a room with a door and one window, or hole in the wall about one foot square. It was not flooded with light that would dazzle one's eyes, nor cause one to bother about the black mud-brick walls or dirt floor, yet it was a shelter, and what more could one want in winning souls? On the last Sunday of the campaign, I was preaching to a very full church; and as I gave the alter call, I asked the people to move back from the altar three or four feet to make room for seekers. Men and women sit on opposite sides of the church in Egypt, with a short wall in between, and the men on their side of the church were coming to the front to commit their lives to the Lord. All at once, I saw a policeman's rifle being tossed across the church to a fellow, and that policeman and others making a bee-line for the altar. He knelt right in front of where my wife was standing on the platform. We went to prayer, and as Hazel was praying for him, a tear from her eyes fell on his hand. Many times, I have heard him tell about it; that tear falling on his hand broke up the fountain of his heart, and he wept his way to a believing relationship with Jesus Christ as his Saviour. His brother, the one to whom he threw his rifle, also was saved before that meeting was over. A good number joined the church from that campaign.

We were also in Dermowas, which was known as a wicked town. When the uprising against the British took place in 1919, a mob in Dermowas stopped the train from going through to Cairo, because they knew that train held a number of British soldiers. They took the soldiers off the train, killed them, cut their bodies into pieces, put them in hand carts and went through the streets calling out, "British meat for sale."

When the uprising was put down within a couple of days, the British brought the ringleaders of the mob to justice and death was meted out to them. The pastor of Dermowas told me that story, and said, "This is a very hard place in which to do much for the Lord." We spent nearly three weeks there. On Friday of the second week, we had an all day meeting with fasting and praying. That night, the break came, and souls began seeking the Lord. One man got saved while I was preaching. He jumped to his feet, gave a good testimony of what the Lord had done for him right there while he was still in his chair. The pastor told me that in the next days, around twenty-five were saved. Praise be to God!

"BLIND BAKEETA – A GREAT SACRIFICE"

Somewhere around this time in the sequence of the work of the Mission, Brother Black, the Mission Superintendent, received a letter from a women of Ghanaim, a village of forty thousand people, situated near the mountain on the west side of Egypt. In this letter, she told about being in a nearby village called Bagoor. She was blind, and the only way she could make a living was to beg. This poor beggar was passing along a street when she heard singing and enquired what it was. She was told that the 'Islah' (the name given to our mission by the Egyptians in its early days; it means "Reformers") were holding meetings there. She went in, heard the gospel for the first time, and was wonderfully converted. In this letter, she was still begging, but it was for a preacher of God's Word, to be sent to her village of Ghanaim to open meetings such as she had experienced in Bagoor.

The superintendent replied that they had nobody available to send and that they had no extra money to open the work. A short time elapsed, and then another letter came, still begging that the work be opened. The same reply was sent. A third letter came, and in that letter she told us that though she was only a poor, blind beggar, yet in her begging she had saved fifty dollars, and that she would give that fifty dollars to support a preacher, and by the time it was gone, she believed that there would be enough people saved to support a preacher in Ghanaim. We could turn her down no longer. Such faith and such sacrifice demanded our action. Brother Yougeem Gergis, a fine Egyptian preacher, was sent to get a place for meetings; and then I decided that I would go to pioneer a church in that place.

A place was secured. Four mud brick walls and a door was all that we could find. Quartered palm trees were laid from two palm tree posts in the centre of each of the walls, and maize stalks laid over them covered us from the sun. A mud brick platform was built for the preacher. There we began in a new village and in a new place of worship, among an entirely new people, but the Lord had prepared the way through poor, blind Bakeeta's witnessing for Him. After a meeting or two, we had people coming to kneel at that platform to find Jesus. Even though it was just a black, mud altar, precious people received a heaven-born, sky-blue experience that has stood all tests that the devil sent along. I was there for three Sundays and souls were continually plowing through to victory.

The last Sunday, as I was preaching, I noticed quite a fine looking man back in the far corner of the meeting house. He watched us and listened very intently. I gave an altar call and four or five came forward. We prayed, then I asked for testimonies. During the testimonies, the converts became very happy, and while singing some verses of a hymn, suddenly they jumped to their feet, clapped their hands, sang with all their might, and began going around in a large circle. After five minutes, they all fell to their knees, and prayed very earnestly for a time. The man in the far corner watched this whole episode with his eyes bulging from their sockets. When they fell to their knees, he did the same, and prayed back there in his corner with all his heart, asking God to forgive and save him. When the prayers were over, he jumped to his feet, and gave this testimony.

"I am a sorcerer and my little boy has been attending the children's meetings here. He learned some hymns and has been singing them, and begging me to come to hear the foreigner preach. Now the Lord has saved me from my sorcery. Much of my work has been casting so-called Christian devils out of Mohammedan women, but now the Lord has cast the devil out of me."

He was so happy that he clapped his hands with joy. It was a great victory for the Lord's cause, and when I was in Egypt, nearly thirty years later, he still had a glowing testimony for Jesus Christ.

At the close of that day's meetings, I formed a society and took in as members blind Bakeeta and twenty-five men. Some women had found Christ, but they didn't join at the forming of the Society. Those twenty-five men from that very day supported their pastor and Bakeeta too, so she never had to beg again.

In three or four weeks after I had returned to Assiut, I received a request from that same church to come back for another week. It was arranged, and back I went with great joy. We had a good week with more souls finding the Lord.

On Sunday night, after the service, practically all of the brethren came to where I was staying. It was winter time, and I didn't even have corn stalks between myself and the stars, but I was happy, though often at night pretty cold. The spokesman for the brethren came close to me and said, "We want you to stay for another day." I made some excuse and said, "I think I had better go," but he continued, "We want you to stay another day, and in the morning we will all come and begin digging a foundation for a new church. A brother is giving us land for a church." "But," I said, "You don't need me to start building a church." "Oh yes, we do," he continued, "the mayor of the village will come and stop us from building, but not even the devil will wag his tongue if you stay with us." I said, "I don't think the devil is that much afraid of me, but in that case, I will stay for tomorrow."

Bright and early, the brethren all gathered with their digging tools and baskets to carry away the debris from the excavation. They prepared a chair for their "protector" and sat me on it in the midst of the new church property. In about an hour, a crowd of people, soldiers and the mayor came down the streets toward us. They gathered around the brethren as they worked. At last, the mayor said to the pastor, "What are you doing here?" The pastor said, "We are digging a foundation to build a church!" An argument began and the mayor took the pastor by the top of his head and chin, and was shaking him quite vigorously. At that point, I intervened and said to the mayor, "Here, what are you doing to our preacher?" He let the preacher go and turned to me and said, "You can't build a church here." "Oh yes we can, and we are going to build a church right here," I said.

"I won't let you. I will command my guards with their guns to make you stop," the mayor shouted. "Listen," I said, "If you are going to use force to stop us, I will soon show you what we will do." I called to our church members, "Brethren, bring me two donkeys. I am going to Aboutig to lay the matter before the District Chief of Police."

In two or three hours, the donkeys carried me to Aboutig where I met the Chief of Police and told him the whole affair. I asked him to send his police and guard our brethren as they built, but he wouldn't commit himself. I saw an ultimatum was necessary and I stated, "I am going to Assiut, and I will give you until I get to the city to decide what you are going to do. If, by then, there isn't a phone call from you saying you have sent soldiers to guard the brethren while they are building, I will take it to the Governor of the Province."

Just as I was walking into the hallway of the Mission home, the phone rang. I answered it and there was the Chief of Police of the Aboutig district asking for me. The Chief said, "I have complied with your request, and have sent police to guard your men while they build the church." I thanked him very much and the church went forward. The mayor's sprouting wings were well clipped.

When the brethren had finished the church properly, and were finished the living quarters of their pastor, they added an extra room for blind Bakeeta as her place of abode. Numerous times I have seen her sitting contentedly in her room weaving the baskets out of material that the brethren supply for her. They sell the baskets that she makes at the weekly market. Bakeeta is very happy, attends all the meetings, and gives her spoken testimony, even among the men. This is a thing quite out of place for any native woman to do in the villages of Egypt. However, it is all right for Bakeeta, for she is one with special privileges.

In January, 1929, my wife received a cable saying, "Mother gone, Father very ill." Three days later another cable came saying, "Father gone." It was a sad time, but we knew where Hazel's parents were, for they had loved and served the Lord for many years. When my father-in-law, Mr. Pritchard, heard that his dear wife had passed on, he quoted a verse from Job 2:10: "What, shall we receive good at the hand of God, and shall we not receive evil?" The "Evil" was the sickness from which he too was very ill. The "Good" came in being re-united in just three days with his beloved.

In the spring of 1929, March 2, I received a cable telling that my mother had also died. How I missed her weekly letters. I knew that she hadn't been well. She told me about it, but I didn't expect it so soon. I thought that she would live until we would get home the following year, but God took her home to a glorious reward.

We would have been home for all their passings if we could have gone a little earlier for our furlough, but I had been made General Superintendent the previous year when Rev. Black had gone on furlough, so I couldn't go home until the summer of 1930 when Rev. Black returned.

During the fall of 1929, we invited Rev. G.W. Ridout, an American evangelist, to stop off in his trip from the far east and give us time for some preaching missions. he replied from India, saying that he would do so. We made great preparations, putting up a tent that would hold a multitude. That meeting started on Friday morning and ran for five days. The great tent was filled and overflowing three times a day. Some said that there were five thousand people attending the services. Dr. Ridout certainly preached some great messages and a host of people found Jesus as their Lord and Saviour.

AN UNUSUAL CALL TO PREACH

Just about this time, I had a letter from a brother in the Lord, Iyad Gergis, who lived at Akhmin, a city across the Nile river from Suhag, some distance south of Assiut. He was a weaver by trade and a good brother in the church. Quite often he preached very acceptably for his pastor, who was very sick for some months while in that church. In this letter Iyad told of his call to preach the gospel. In substance, it was as follows:

"For some time the Lord has been calling me to preach,

but I have been dilatory about going as I have a good business and don't want to leave it. I was crossing the river to Suhag on business the other day, and as I walked out on the long narrow ramp that takes you to the boat, one of the animals that was being taken across got unruly, jumped, and knocked me off the ramp into deep water a few feet from the boat. I can't swim, so I went to the bottom. While down there the Lord said to me, 'Will you preach if I save your life?' and my answer was, 'Lord, I'll preach.' So I am writing to you to see if you have a charge for me."

I knew him well and felt that he should be preaching, so I answered at once, informing him that we needed a preacher at Beni Smaya, requesting that he go immediately. God blessed his labours abundantly in Beni Smaya. He didn't stay very long preaching in the villages. The city churches were calling for him. Any church in Egypt would be only too happy to have Rev. Iyad Gergis, as their pastor. He is spoken of in Egypt as the orator of the church and he sometimes refers to himself as Jonah, referring to another call to preach that involved some deep water. He is now the Egyptian Superintendent of our church.

Hazel and I had been married over four years before a wee girl, Willa Royce, came along on October 1, 1929, to bless our home. What a blessing she was, especially to her mother, who had just lost both of her parents. She sometimes would say that the Lord had sent Willa along just at the right time to comfort her heart.

The time for our first furlough finally came, and how our hearts beat with anticipation for our beloved Canada and our loved ones there. A ten day stop-over in London was welcome, however, because we were busy every day "doing the town" as the saying goes. We saw a good number of places, historic and modern, coming to a greater appreciation of our Loyalist heritage.

After crossing the Atlantic, we landed at Montreal and then on to Ottawa, where quite a crowd had gathered to welcome us and take us home with them. On our way, we stopped at the cemetery in Elgin, Ontario, where my mother had been laid to rest. As I stood beside that grave, sad in heart, it came to me so forcibly, "Mother is not here, she is in heaven." I left the graveside and cemetery, still missing Mother, but thanking the Lord that she was not there, but in heaven, and that some day, in the will of the Lord, I would meet her over there.

When I left home for Egypt, Mother kissed me and said, "Goodbye," at the side door of the house. When we got out onto the road in front of the house, Mother was standing in the front doorway waving to me, her last earthly goodbye. There was no earthly welcome home from her now as we drove into the yard nearly eight years later, yet it felt good to be in the home where she had lived and loved for over forty years. Even though more than a year had gone by since Mother's death, Father was still lonely and helpless, as she had looked after everything around the house, and even helped him to dress in his Sunday clothing. My brother, Stuart, had come home from the West before Mother had passed away, and he looked after the housekeeping. He was very capable and continued at home until he bought a farm of his own about a mile away.

The following summer, my youngest brother, Eddie, decided to marry Miss Elsie Frayn and she agreed, so it was my privilege to bind them together. Eddie and Elsie took over the home and Father lived with them for over eight years until he was taken to his eternal home on January 2, 1940. I was in Egypt again, and alone again, when Father died, but I am getting ahead of myself in the story.

The fall of 1930, September 22, the Lord added to us another daughter, Elaine Joy. She was brought to the light of this world in the Salvation Army Hospital in Ottawa. More joy was ours, not just in her name, but in our hearts.

That year, I did much Missionary deputational work, visiting churches and camp meetings on behalf of the missionary cause, trying to share the heavy missionary burden with our supporters.

In the fall of 1931, we planned going back to the Mission field, but the Board thought that we had better wait another year. We complied with their request, thinking for the children's sakes that it might be better. Rev. P. Wiseman, who had been my Bible College Principal, now was Superintendent. I asked him if there was any church vacant, where we might be appointed until the following summer. His reply was "You could to go Shawville, Quebec, if you wish." I prayed earnestly, spoke to Hazel about it and decided we would go. We immediately packed up and moved into the Shawville parsonage. Rev. Wiseman had told us that the work was rather low. Nevertheless, we prayed much, visited a lot and it began to pick up. In January, we arranged for Miss Evangeline Warren, a beautiful soloist, to come to sing in revival meetings, while I did the preaching. After six weeks of revival services with preaching every night, it was decided to have a three day convention. Following the convention, we even carried on the services one more week. Many received definite conversion experiences.

God and I were in the church one night, all alone, after the regular service was over. What a wonderful time I had in praying through for two people, who didn't find God during the campaign, but did the next summer. We can pray the prayer of faith and the work is as good as if it were already accomplished.

The following summer, we left Shawville, attended several camp meetings, and prepared to go to Egypt, sailing from New York on a tourist boat. It was a marvellous trip. The boat stopped for one or two days each at most of the important ports of the Mediterranean Sea and two of the Black Sea Ports, Istanbul and Constanza. We were forty-two days touring before it reached Alexandria, Egypt. What a beautiful experience. It prepared and rested Hazel and myself for the trying time ahead.

Chapter Eight

"Brick Over The Wall"

This second time we were quite at home in Alexandria and in due time we made our way to Cairo, and on to Assiut. Shortly after our arrival, we decided to go to Minia, and divide the country as to evangelism, our part being from Mallawi, north to Alexandria. So it was ordered, and we took up our abode in the apartment, just above the Minia church, while Rev. Saad Gholerial, the native pastor, had the third storey apartment for his living quarters.

As soon as we arrived, we started revival services in the Minia Church. Prevailing prayer brought victory in those special services. One medical doctor, who attended the services regularly, said to me one night after a great meeting, "Before you start to preach, you look pale and sick, but when you get preaching, you look hale and hearty." I have no doubt that this was the power of the Holy Spirit coming on me which energized me both in spirit and in body.

Shortly after that series of meetings, Minia city officials told us they were taking a whole block, including our church, for some city buildings. We set our price, and would not come down any lower. We felt that it was worth our named price, so after all the other buildings were torn down, they came along and paid us our price. This left us in possession until we could build a very fine new church and living apartments, both for the native pastor's family and our own. It fell to me to oversee the building of that church and the living quarters. At the same time, I was in evangelistic services in nearby villages, where God blessed abundantly.

During the year we stayed in Minia, I kept a record of the souls saved in the revival meetings. There were five hundred and forty-two converted and received into church membership. Most of the converts over there still stand true to the Lord.

In one place that year, where God gave us a gracious revival, some persecution was experienced. We were holding the services out on a dead-end street. No place was big enough to hold the crowds of people. At the time, we had no church in that particular village and this was a pioneer effort. Every night, after we had preached, we would give an invitation to seekers to go into the sitting room of the house beside us, then we would dismiss the crowd and go in to help the seekers to find the One who is seeking for them. One night as we were preaching, a brick came sailing over a wall. No doubt it was meant for me, but it just missed me and hit my interpreter right on his chest. For just a moment, he held his chest, then we went on as though nothing had happened. Surely, the devil was mightily stirred over the loss of souls to his satanic realm. Not long after that, a good church building was constructed in that village.

While we were living in the old church in Minia, our two girls got amoeba dysentry. We took them to the hospital in Assiut, where doctors would treat them and they would be fine for awhile but the sickness would soon return. Around the first of July 1933, Willa, our older girl was sick with it again, so we left her in bed. The next morning when I lifted her in my arms, she was just as limp as a rag. I carried her, running across to the next block to the English hospital. The doctor hurried, took a big needle, and injected a quart of salt water into her body. Other treatments were given for a few days and she picked up and was fine through the remainder of the summer.

In September, we went back to Minia, and sporadically the girls were in the American hospital in Assiut. The doctors said at last, "If you want to save Willa's life, you will have to get her out of this country." We relayed the doctor's verdict to the Missionary Board. They said, "Come on home." In May, 1934, we took Willa out of the hospital, took the train for Port Said to the Peniel School, where we stayed a day or two and then boarded the freighter, which was sailing for Halifax. Willa was thin, pale and sickly when we went aboard ship, but before we got to Halifax, the sea air had kissed roses back into her cheeks, and health to her whole body. How happy it made her mother and dad.

When we arrived in Halifax, I immediately went to the Post Office for mail, because our Canadian Superintendent had informed me that he would send our half fare travel booklets to Halifax. I got the booklets and a letter telling me that we had been given a church in Smith Falls, Ontario and could send our luggage right there. By the time I got back to the ship, I was sick, weaving like a drunk man as I walked. I said to one of the boat's officers, "I guess I am land sick. Would you make me a cup of tea?" I drank it and was immediately better. I never was sea-sick, but I certainly was land sick on that occasion.

We moved into the parsonage of the Smith's Falls Church, and were we ever happy to have both Elaine and Willa well again. The people were so good to us too. One dear old brother said to us one day as we were visiting at their home, "I don't see how you can be so bubbling over with joy all of the time." I couldn't help but say, "It is because the Lord is so good to us."

At Lombardy, an additional preaching point of the Smith's Falls circuit, we put on a revival campaign for some weeks. Miss Alice Stevens, now Mrs. Corneil, was over as our special singer, and I did the preaching as I had done previously in Shawville, Quebec. Some gracious victories were recorded in heaven in that campaign. A good number who were saved during that meeting are still serving the Lord, as are their growing families.

God's work was done in the Smith's Falls Church and our congregation steadily increased. After being there two happy years, and much against the people's wishes, we were moved to Campbell's Bay, Quebec, in July 8, 1936. There wasn't the outlet for a person's labours there in the little Quebec village that there was in Smith's Falls.

A blessed event occured one month after moving to Quebec. It was the birth of our son. Many a prayer had been offered up for the Lord to give us a boy, and the Lord answered. We named him David Charles.

After being in Campbell's Bay for two years, the Lord laid His calling on me again at the Quebec district camp meeting. The voice said, "I want you to go back to Egypt again." Our Superintendent felt the same way about it, so on the first of September, we left Campbell's Bay and moved into the little home at Ramsayville, Ontario, near Ottawa, where my wife's father and mother had built a house when they left the farm at Alcove, Quebec. We planned that I should go over alone the first year and see what arrangements could be made for the children's education. Hazel and the children were to follow me a year later, but I didn't like the looks of the international situation and wasn't sure what could happen. Canada was the safest for my family.

Arrangements were made with the Missionary Board that my wife was to get twenty dollars a month for herself and the three children to live on, and five dollars a month to pay her small rent to her sister and brother-in-law, Mr. and Mrs. Harvey Lindsay. They owned the little house that Hazel's parents had built for their retirement. On the Mission field, I received the same money as other missionaries, five dollars a month over and above room and board. Hardly enough to get rich quickly.

This is part of Dad's letter to Mother written just after the news of his Father's death.

Rosecut 22/9/39

My Darling Hazel

It is nearly a week now since I sent Willie's letter, so I will get at one for my precious far away wife. It makes me lonesome to think that you would have been here in seven or eight days now if this awful war had not started. Now there is no telling when it may end. It looks as though it were nearly an end in Poland with both Germany & Russia at her. Poor Poland bleeds to death right to a finish the best of Hitler, luck it is not that an evil yet. And may God grant she may be freed from tyranny & heel and the tyrants forevertasting

I wrote letters to each & my brothers since the death of father. I am praying God to bless them & the God of their souls. Paul I long to see them face their hearts to Jesus so that, as Father and Mother as often prayed, the family circle would be unbroken. It would be an awful thing to have Louisone & and so know they are not saved. Did you write to my neighbor as you said you were going to do? or thinking of doing? Well Dear I can't think of anymore just now to write to the best lady in all the world, so I will call a half here for now, or when I say this. I just wish you were no farther off than ... there is. There is one great comfort now in writing, so Khaky and the is that you don't have to stay in his house, column again. this stage is a grand place to rest. She would be very happy as there to either. Monday I got journey came when I came up from Salomon with mother picture in it. I ...

52

Canadian Mission

Rev. R. L. MAINSE

Superintendent

ASSIOUT, Egypt.

كنيسة
(بيرت القداسة الكنيسة)
للدير : القس متّر
بسيوط

6/1/40.

My Darling Haidie:

Well I waited for the mail to come in this morning to see if any come from you ere I sent this off. but none come as I will start this across the waters that separate me from my loving wife. We are not playing the part of husband and wife very well that day or we, but you my dear are playing the part of mother real well I know for as please your and we will continue to love each other through there is no visible way of showing it. If I had known things were going to turn out as they did, I would never have promised to come without your. However, Bye-bye for now with lots of love, hugs [x]

Ray

PUBLISHER'S NOTE
I am sharing a few of Dad's poems which were written around and during the years of separation. The
one entitled "Sonny" is most meaningful to me.

March 29, 1944, Assiut, Egypt

'SONNY'

Now that's what I feel to call you,
You, whom I'll love my whole life through.
Sonny's a bright and cheery name,
And is 'Daddy' to you the same?
A good son is a precious gift,
To the father who needs a lift,
When the pathway of life seems hard,
And e'en would his foot-steps retard.

O' that nippy hop, step and jump,
Which does not lack pep at the pump,
Puts courage and vim in us all,
And helps us rise up should we fall.
May your teen-age be bright and gay,
As you march forth to manhood's day;
Be e'er free from evil design,
Be full of kindness to mankind.

To future with promise is bright,
To you, if you dare to do right;
'Twill to you in life grant a place,
Where you'll never no, ne'er lose face;
E'en among the true and renowned,
Who did fight and have won the crown,
That shall never more fade away
In that haven of endless day.

So my dear son it's up to you,
To trust in God and ever do,
That which is good, and better still,
Follow the leadings of His will:
Yea, follow the gleam from afar,
And for His best do thou aspire!
Blest help Divine will God vouchsafe
To every stray, prodigal waif.

A HERO

If you can meet crushing defeat,
In some great plan of life,
Then take on courage to repeat
A new plan without strife.

If you can face the sea-horse wild,
White manes, with foaming breath;
And treat it as an angry child,
In spite of seeming death.

If you can break your passions strong,
When they your mind consume;
And won't do it because it's wrong,
And brings black hellish doom.

If you can think thoughts good and pure,
When sin does flout and surge,
Then you're a bloke who shall endure,
When your Judge makes His purge.

If you to evil an say no,
Like the Christ of Calv'ry,
When temptations around you blow,
Then ver'ly you are free.

YES. I'M COMING

I am coming on a cloud,
With no sorrow and no shroud,
For my Lord I am to meet,
And won't I just kiss His feet,
Till He lifts me by His hand
And bids me before Him stand.

I am coming with out a shout,
Having won yon earthly bout,
With the enemy of souls:
While eternity does roll,
I will make Christ's praises known,
As to me they have been shown.

I am coming on that day
When the Lord, His church shall pay,
For its perfect loyalty.
Then the Judge of royalty,
Will His priests and kings reward,
With the glory of their Lord.

I am coming so look for me,
O'er flowing with very glee;
Mounting up on eagle's wings,
Loosing sight of earthly things;
Christ is all in all to me,
And I am forever free.

Chapter Nine

"The Waters That Separate"

About two weeks after we moved to Ramsayville, I said farewell to my wife and three children, for what I thought might be one year at the most. It became six and one half years of separation. Miss M. Cooke, a lady missionary, my nephew, Lorne Kenny and I boarded a boat at Montreal for La Harve, France. A couple of days were spent in Paris, then on to Marseilles where we took another ship for Alexandria. The train took us again to Cairo and Assiut. Before another year rolled around, the second world war had broken out, and there was no possibility of Hazel and the children getting to Egypt. They were safer at home in Canada anyway, for there were troublesome times in Egypt.

Bombing raids were continually carried out on Port Said and Alexandria and sometimes Cairo. During the war, we went each summer to Port Said for a rest from the awful heat of Upper Egypt. We escaped much of the heat, but one night we were suddenly aroused from our slumber by midnight sirens. For two or three hours, search lights flashed, heavy guns boomed, flares were dropped, and then we heard the whistle of the bombs. When we heard that whistle, we would dash for our shelter in the basement of the school. At the bursting of that string of bombs, we would come out and watch the awesome beauty of the fireworks again. It was a strenuous and trying time indeed.

The following year, we had just arrived at Port Said

for a few days, when the news came that the Germans and the Italians had driven the British back to Alemain. The British Consul in Port Said informed us that we had better get away to the south, or we might be shut in there. Being Mission Superintendent, I felt we had better go back up the country to Assiut and on to the Sudan, so that we could fly to the West coast of Africa from there if need arose. By July 11, 1943, we were at Khartoum, in the Sudan, where our dear elderly sister, Miss E.A. Burke, had been for years. The C.M.S. Mission had a vacant house in Omdurman, across the Nile River from Khartoum, which they freely put at our disposal for our stay there. We were very thankful to the C.M.S. for their great kindness to us. We came back from the Sudan in relays, but all arrived safely and we were in Egypt for General Montgomery's great counter-offensive. the Christians of Egypt prayed much for Montgomery and rejoiced exceedingly over his great victories.

By the fall of 1944, the Nazis were driven out of North Africa and almost out of the Mediterranean area. It seemed a possibility to get home to Canada. I wrote to the Missionary Board. They gave me permission to go home, and so by the middle of October, I had boarded a ship in Port Said.

We joined a convoy and started west. Off the coast near Alexandria, more ships joined us. Our boat left the convoy and went into Algiers. For three days they unloaded our cargo of tea until the ship was about half unloaded. The rest of the tea was for New Brunswick. After the unloading, we pulled away from the pier and anchored a couple of miles offshore where we stayed for one whole week until the next convoy came along. We then steamed out and joined it. There were around forty ships crossing the Atlantic together. A couple of times, we had submarine warnings, but nothing came of it. The ships surely did some manoeuverings. It was very interesting to behold their anti-torpedo tactics.

Thoughts of Hazel, my daughters and son filled my

mind. Joy and excitement caused poetry to flow from my soul. Here are some I wrote while on board ship.

"Poems on board ship"

Nov. 10, 1944 Atlantic Ocean

A STORM AT SEA

Three days ago the wind began to blow,
At first it blew softly, the waves did grow
Till they rocked our boat, and pitched it about,
As though 'twere a bee on a camel's snout.

The storm came riding prancing white-maned steeds,
Tossing head and mane with foamy wee beads
From a frothy mouth that's ne'er satisfied,
Lest it can swallow ships where'er they're spied.

Up, up we go on the crest of the wave,
Down, down we descend as into a cave;
The billows around, o'er us try to roll,
Making us think of Heaven and the soul.

Now, in Heav'n no storm shall ruffle its sea,
Throughout the ages of eternity;
All shall be calm and so peaceful up there,
For it is the home that we all may share.

So billows may roll while ships rise and fall,
We're trusting in Christ the Master of all:
We'll sail the wide sweeps of time's stormy seas,
Until He says 'Halt' to the salt-scented breeze.

Then we shall take wing like an albatross,
Forsaking this world and all of its dross,
To realms that are free from sin and its shame,
Where Jesus is all in all like His Name.

A PAEAN OF PRAISE

O praise the Lord, I love Him well,
I love Him more than tongue can tell;
I love His face, I love His feet,
The place where all the world may meet.

Glory to God I am the Lord's,
I am the servant of His words;
I am for Him and He's for me,
O'er yonder on dark Calvary.

Hallelujah, I know His grace,
I know also His smiling face;
I know the day when He forgave,
The sins of this benighted slave.

Glory, glory, I now am free,
I'm free in thought in word, in deed,
Free to live for the Christ, who died,
Who to my heart His blood applied,

IF

'If' is a word of great import,
But of such dwarfish dimensions,
Using the future to support
Its great and varied intentions.
'If' is a fact like a barn-door hinge,
On which our movements seem to swing,
And we are no doubt hindering
Our best laid plans ere they can wing
Their way into the world of things,
Where they can claim to be a fact,
On which the future thus may act,
And discard "If" forevermore
Among the gods of old folk-lore.

OUR TWENTIETH WEDDING ANNIVERSARY

'Twas twenty years ago today,
That Hazel and I, young and gay,
Stood side by side at altar rails,
And pledged ourselves to never fail,
One the other while time should last,
As we sail thro' time's fiery blast.

Two-thirds of those years we did spend,
Always together ere I did wend
Back to Egypt's dark, needy land,
Where she and I had joined our hands,
To walk the path of live as one,
Serving our Lord, God's only Son.

More than six years has passed between
This day and that, when last my queen
Bade me God's speed and I set sail,
Planning her coming without fail,
Within the space of one long year,
When she and our three would appear.

Now I am on my journey home,
No more alone to ever roam;
God being my Helper, I'll stay
With my help – meet in the good way,
That the Lord has marked out for us
To walk therein with Christ Jesus.

Nov. 21, 1944 Bay of Fundy

REVELATION OF GOD

Could there an act upon this earth,
Ever compare with Jesus' birth?
When He was born a little Child,
So sweet and lovely, meek and mild.

Rings there a bell than can arouse
The man of sin who does carouse,
Around the very brink of hell,
Where forever the damned shall dwell?

Writes there a scribe on parchment white;
Who's refused to walk in the light
Of inspiration from above;
And miss the fact that "God is love"?

Reads there a man with eyes so blind;
That in God's word he cannot find
The path that forth to duty leads,
Where God's supply will meet your needs?

Dec. 12, 1944

DOUBT AND FAITH.

"Doubt sees the obstacles –
Faith sees the way
Doubt sees the darkest night –
Faith sees the day
Doubt dreads to take a step –
Faith soars on high
Doubt questions, "Who believes?"
Faith answers, "I"."

About two days out from New York, our ship broke off from the convoy, and started alone for St. John, N.B. We ran into the worst storm I have ever seen. Shortly after leaving the convoy, the captain of the ship and the chief wireless operator were thrown right out of their bunks by the waves and onto the floor. I, the only passenger, had the hospital room. It was a swing bed and continually bumped both sides of the cabin. My trunks were in my room and were rumbling back and forth across the floor and under the bed. I couldn't sleep, so I got up, put my clothes on and started for the dining saloon. When I opened the door and went in, I was sent scooting right across the room, landing against the far wall with my hand on the button of the Chief Steward's bell, which rang and rang until I realized I was ringing the bell. I didn't try to sleep anymore that night. In talking to the captain the next morning, he said to me, "A storm like that would make you think of praying." I quite agreed with the captain, that it would. We braved the storm and made it to St. John on November 21, 1944. It was a beautiful sunny morning, but around 4:00 p.m., as we were leaving St. John by train, it began to snow. When we got to Ottawa, the next morning, we had around five inches of the white stuff. That was quite normal for Canada, but it wasn't normal for a fellow just coming home from Egypt.

On arrival in Ottawa, since nobody knew I was coming, I phoned Hazel at Ramsayville and, for the first time in over six years, I heard her dear voice. She phoned my eldest daughter who was attending Lisgar High School in Ottawa. Soon I saw a fine looking young lady coming down the steps of the Union Station. I just didn't recognize her, but I said to myself, "I'll go walking over towards her." When we were still twenty-five feet from each other, we recognized each other and our greetings were very happy. What a change there was in Willa from a girl of ten to a young lady of sixteen.

Before long, Hazel's brother, Rev. M.C. Pritchard, came and another happy greeting followed. The three of us set off for Ramsayville. When we drove into the yard, there stood my dear wife. She said, as we greeted each other after over six years apart, "Here in this very spot you left me. Here I am when you come back." Elaine and David, our other two children were attending Ramsayville Public School, and I didn't see them until the noon hour.

From the 22nd of November, when I arrived home, until the first few days of January, I had a holiday with my family. During those holidays, the trustees of Ramsayville Public School came to me, asking me to take over the fifty-two pupil school for the rest of the school year. They said that the school inspector had given his sanction to their hiring me. An agreement was reached and I became a school master for six enjoyable months, teaching Elaine and David, my two youngest. The only thing that I didn't enjoy was the sciatica rheumatism I received coming right out of a hot country into the cold, cold winter of our Canada.

The pain tormented me from the first part of January until Easter Sunday afternoon. I was called upon to dismiss the Sunday afternoon service of the Young People's Easter Convention which was held in the Fifth Avenue Church in Ottawa. What a hard time I had to get to my feet because of the sciatica, but while praying, the blessing of high Heaven flooded my soul, and the resurrection life of Christ completely healed me. It was so bad that the sides of my limbs and the heels of my feet were sore like a boil, but in one second I was perfectly well. Praise His dear Name!

That summer of 1945, I was asked by the Eastern Canada Superintendent, Rev. J.C. Black, if I would take a church at the Ontario village of Madoc. I agreed and just before school opened, we moved to Madoc. We had a very good fall and winter there, saw some fruit of our labours, and met a lot of fine people.

Around the first of June, 1946, I had a communication from the Annesley College Board asking me to become the Principal of the College. After considerable thought and prayer, I agreed. I was officially appointed as Principal of Annesley College from that time. We moved most of our belongings to Annesley College the first of June but lived in Kingston until September 1, when we went to Ottawa to prepare the College for its October 1 opening. During the summer, I travelled to all the camp meetings representing Annesley College and encouraged students to yield to the call of God for labourers in His work.

The College Board asked, in the spring of 1947, if I would consider going to Winona Lake School of Theology's summer course. I told them that I would be delighted to do so. There I started a theological course which I continued until receiving my Bachelors, my Masters and finally, my Doctors degree in Theology.

The majority of the College Board felt that a merger of the two institutions, Annesley College and Brockville Bible College, would be very beneficial and might hasten a union of the two church groups. We approached the Brockville officials and they were favourable towards the proposition. Official arrangements were made for our Annesley College students to attend the Brockville Bible School, and there in the fall of 1948, we put the Annesley College property up for sale. Before long it was sold to an Ottawa automobile dealership.

"BACK INTO PASTORAL WORK"

Around September 1, 1948, we took an appointment of two churches, Haleys and Admaston, which are country charges near Renfrew in the Ottawa Valley. A little over three months after our arrival, my wife took sick on December 8. I called a doctor in Renfrew, and he said to bring her down to the hospital. She spent a week there and was getting much worse, so he said that I would have to take her by ambulance to Ottawa. There she spent thirty-three days.

When she entered the Ottawa Civic Hospital, she was at first in a semi-private room, which had four beds. On the day when I entered her room, she looked in great distress. I was quite alarmed and asked her if I could do anything for her. She whispered, "I can't stand the tobacco smoke." I said, "I'll get you into a private room." A room was soon secured, and she no longer had to breathe second-hand tobacco smoke, nor first-hand smoke either.

Hazel wanted Willa, Elaine, David and I to spend Christmas Day with her, so we arranged to do so. She made it a very happy time for us all. She was so cheerful. Presents were exchanged and our last Christmas together was like former Christmases, sweet and heavenly. The only thing that marred it was that she was in a sick bed.

She gradually got worse and worse until they said that they would have to move her into another room, which was certainly not as nice and cheerful. I called for four or five elders of the church to come and anoint her according to the scriptures in James five. She seemed better after that for a couple of days, but then she got worse again. I was staying with her every night. One night, she was suffering very acutely, I said to her, "Hazel, would you like me to especially pray for you?" She answered that she would. I stood by her bed of suffering and prayed. God surely came down in blessing. When I opened my eyes, I beheld the most beautiful sight of Hazel that could possibly be. Her beautiful countenance was transfigured. It was aglow with Heaven. The only thing that I can compare it to was the countenance of those I saw in the vision of Heaven which I had as a young man. In three or four minutes, the glow and the outshining glory began to fade. From that time, for the days she remained with us, she had no more pain or suffering.

On Saturday, January 15, she seemed better than she had been. She thought she would be all right and that I could go back to my churches and take my Sunday services, coming to the hospital after the Sunday night service. I spoke to the doctor and he said that it would be all right to do so. About 4:00 p.m. on Sunday afternoon, the phone rang and the message was, "Come at once, and bring the children." We got ready as quickly as possible. I drove as fast as I dared over the treacherous January roads. By 7:00 p.m. we were there. Two nurses were working over her to keep her there until we arrived. As soon as we stepped into the room, they took their instruments and went out.

When we had all gathered into the room, Hazel looked around upon us, and then did her utmost to tell us something. After she had finished speaking she gave two or three gasps and was gone to be with her

Lord. David, twelve years of age, standing at the foot of her bed, raised his hand and very emphatically said, "I'll meet you in heaven, Mother, I will, I will." Truly that was and is the determination of all of us. David was quite sure that Hazel had called his name in her last attempt to speak.

Mr. Robert Code, of Haleys, told a very unusual experience that very night, shortly after Mrs. Mainse had passed away. He was trying to sleep, and all of a sudden, Mrs. Mainse appeared in his bedroom, exhorted him to get saved and to give his heart to the Lord. Then she disappeared, but he never got away from that exhortation, and about three or four months later, he and Mrs. Code were wonderfully saved in our Haley's Church. What a blessing they were to the church and to its pastor.

Hazel was with her Lord, whom she had loved and served so faithfully and well. As a minister, I would say that if ever there was a saint of God, she was one indeed. In the twenty-four years of our married life, I never heard her say one word out of place. She would never criticize anybody, but would always try to help everyone to her Lord. How often she would stay behind when we would be out visiting and have a confidential, spiritual talk with someone for a few moments. Her life spoke very loudly for the Lord Jesus Christ and, therefore, her words had great effect upon those to whom she spoke.

The work at both appointments went well during my pastorate in the Ottawa Valley. Some souls at both places were saved and added to the church. Thanks be unto God for all that was accomplished. The dear people there were exceedingly good to us.

We were exactly three years on the circuit. A year before I left, I married my daughter Elaine to Glenn Thompson of Buffalo, New York, and ten days before we left Haley's, I married my older daughter Willa, to Harold Hodgins of Pembroke, Ontario.

Chapter Ten

"Get Out of This Country"

On September 10, 1951, with my fifteen year old son, David, as best man, I was married to Miss Elva Bishop, whose mother had been a fine lady evangelist and whose father had lived and died a great preacher. Elva had done a fine work for Missions through the "Crusade for Dimes." She had pushed this fund raising program and had been responsible for raising a great deal of money in support of our missionary work in several countries.

Later that fall, Elva and I left for the Mission field in Egypt. The summer just past, Rev. J.C. Black, one of God's great missionaries, had died suddenly. I was sent over again as Superintendent of the Egyptian work. Times were exceedingly strenuous over there. The Mohammedan government was anything but helpful. They were trying to make it impossible to open up new churches, and they even closed some places that were already open. Their regulations concerning schools were almost impossible to be complied with at all. On top of that, placards were posted in prominent places reading, "Kill the English, they are our enemies." Different times I rubbed the following words off our painted garage doors, "You are donkeys. We will kill you!"

On November 11, 1952, I began my last week's evangelistic preaching in the land of Egypt. It was at a village called Nazelton Milk, which is about twenty-five miles from Assiut. I was driving out every evening, having supper with the pastor before the meeting, then leaving for Assiut right after the service was over. God gave us some wonderful victories practically every night and especially the Sunday of November 16, when I was with them. The pastor told me afterwards when he came to the hospital to see me, that from that week's meetings, he received into the church twenty-five new members. It made me feel that my labours were not in vain in the Lord's work. Much of one's labours with the Government authorities those days seemed in vain, or at least little was accomplished, but not so in the Lord's work.

One Monday in November, I went to a village to preach a convention, only to find that the church had been closed by the order of the Chief of Police. Because of the lack of wisdom of one of our young, inexperienced pastors, an offended Moslem man had gone to the Chief of Police and said that if a convention was allowed to be held in their village, there would be bloodshed. the Chief of Police, instead of sending a couple of police to see that nothing like that happened, sent a number of police to hinder our having a convention and closed the church. I returned to Assiut and met the deputy governor of the Assiut Province, but it was of no use. I went to Cairo, met with the Minister of the Interior and also with Mohammed Niguib, the Prime Minister of Egypt, and the general who headed the coup which ousted King Farouk. He made wonderful promises, but they didn't persuade the Chief of Police to open the church and my trip was in vain. Tired and weary, I returned to Assiut. Just after entering the Mission home about 5:00 p.m., the phone rang, wanting me to go to Nipheila, about twenty-five miles away, to settle a quarrel. I told the pastor that I was tired and that I couldn't go until the next evening. I never got going to settle that quarrel as, the next day, I suffered a "coronary occlusion" around breakfast time.

In the face of all these problems, and the frustration of trying to deal with the Egyptian Government, and along with the care of all of the churches, and preaching nearly every night and twice on Sundays, I had a coronary thrombosis on November 18, 1952 at my breakfast table. I walked about fifteen feet to our bedroom, threw myself on the bed, called to Elva, and asked her to call the doctor.

In a few minutes, a doctor was at my bedside, sticking a hypodermic needle into my arm. The next morning, I got up, went to the bathroom and back to bed, but in a few minutes, we had to call the doctor again. From that time, I was not out of bed for four weeks, except to be taken by ambulance to the American Hospital on the third day after my heart attack.

Trying indeed were those days of complete rest and placidity. I was not even allowed to feed myself, and if I tried to loosen the bed covers with my feet, I would suffer for that bit of exertion. The first day I was in hospital, a male orderly came into my room saying that he was to give me a bath. He started roughly at my head to make a suds like a hand full of cotton just plucked from the cotton brush. I said in Arabic to him, "What do you think you are doing?" "Oh," he said, "I am going to bath you." I answered, "If this is the way you are going to bath me, you are finished right now." He went out and told Miss Mildred Cooke, who was a nurse there, that I would not let him bath me. She came in and wanted to know what the matter was that bothered me. I told her what the orderly had done. She said, "Oh, that is the way they do it with the Egyptians. He won't bother you anymore." From that time, Mrs. Mainse bathed me daily, and it was done perfectly.

After six weeks in the hospital, the doctor said that I could go home. I didn't go home on my own locomotion, but was helped by Mrs. Mainse and my nephew, Lorne Kenny. For four weeks, I was convalescent and was doing my office work for the last few days. Finally, I thought I would like to go up to the right side top apartment and see how the workmen were getting along finishing it up for occupation. I went up those long stairs with one arm around my wife's neck and the other arm on the servant's shoulder, so that they could bear part of my weight. In about two hours, my heart began to miss beats badly. The doctor was called and I was commanded to stay right in bed. I stayed in bed but gradually became worse until the doctor decided that I would have to go back into the hospital. I could feed myself, but I had to stay in bed for a time. Progress towards recovery was slow. After a little over four weeks in hospital, the doctor came into my room and said, "We have decided that the best thing for you to do, if you want to get better, is to get out of this country and go back to Canada!"

Cables passed between Canada and Egypt on this matter. Permission was granted by the Mission Board and plans were made speedily for our flight home to Canada. My wife packed up and we left Assiut by car Saturday morning, March 21, 1953. Lorne Kenny was driving, Mrs. J.C. Black and Mrs. Mainse were in the front with him, while I was lying in the back seat on pillows.

"A MIRACLE OF GOD ACCORDING TO HIS PROMISE"

Just previous to my leaving the hospital for the trip to Canada, I asked the Lord to give me a portion of His word for the trip home, as I was somewhat fearful of such a trip in my condition. The Lord said unto me, more clearly than any human could utter it, "I will give you the one hundred and twenty-first Psalm." I said to myself "What is that Psalm?" I could not think of any of it, so I reached from my bed to the little table for my Bible. I opened the blessed Book and read, "I will lift up mine eyes unto the hills, from whence cometh my help. My help cometh from the Lord, which made heaven and earth. He will not slumber. Behold, He that keepeth Israel shall neither slumber nor sleep. The Lord is thy keeper: the Lord is thy shade upon thy right hand. The sun shall not smite thee by day, nor the moon by night. The Lord shall preserve thee from all evil. He shall preserve thy soul. The Lord shall preserve thy going out and thy coming in from this time forth, and even forevermore."

When I read down to "The Lord is thy keeper," I got so blessed and happy that I was shouting my Lord's praises. After a few minutes of praising the Lord, I read on until I read the last verse, "The Lord shall preserve thy going out and thy coming in from this time forth, and even forevermore." Truly, I went to praising the Lord with greater gusto than before, but I didn't seemingly disturb the hospital very much, because I was in the front room, which was well away from all others.

With my Psalm memorized, it was in my head as well as my heart, I faced the future with great courage. The first obstacle I met was that blazing hot March sun that I could not bear. After telling the folk in the front seat of the car that I could not bear the heat of the sun, I thought of my Psalm and said to the Lord, "Now, Lord, you said to me in the Psalm you gave me, 'The sun shall not smite thee by day.'" Now at that time of year, one does not expect to see clouds in the Egyptian sky. In November or December you will see clouds, but not in March.

After I reminded the Lord of that portion of my Psalm, I don't think it was more than five or ten minutes until the whole sky was clouded over. Not a cloud was there before, and for the next five or six hours, until we entered the suburbs of Cairo, it remained cloudy. As we entered Cairo, my nephew, Lorne Kenny, said, "The sun has just come out now." I know it was the Lord who sent those clouds over us, just as He did for the children of Israel in their wilderness journey. It wasn't just a chance. It was the ordering of my Almighty Lord. Praise be to His Name, His Blessed Holy Name! He will never hear the end of my praises for that Psalm. I quote it over daily and some days many times. I thank and praise Him after nearly each verse as I quote it. It was great when the Lord gave it to me, and it is always growing more precious. I simply love it as from my loving Lord. It is my Psalm still.

In Cairo, we went to a hotel where we stayed from Saturday mid-afternoon until Monday when Lorne took us to the airport to catch the plane at 10:00 p.m. As I was being taken in a wheelchair out to the plane, Mrs. Mainse was walking beside me. We noticed the full moon, and she quoted my Psalm, "Nor the moon by night," and it was reassurance for the trip by plane. A couple of men carried me into the plane and soon all was in readiness. The engines began to roar and away we were, flying as a bird of the night.

In the early morning, we arrived in Rome, stopped for an hour, and then we flew away, seemingly mounting higher and higher until we were beside the Alp's highest peak, Mount Blanc. Seeing Mount Blanc caused me to get my pencil and paper out and begin to write:

"Over the Alps by aeroplane
On a bright and sunny day
It calls to your heart as well as brain,
And makes you truly say –
What a wonder of creative art
Those mountain peaks display!
Cathedral spires fail to impart,
The glory of that day.

The mountain peaks far round and wide
Raised steeples in the air.
Ah! there my soul wished to abide,
And enter them for prayer.
They spoke indeed to my glad heart
The majesty of God –
Yes, hope and faith they did impart,
So God we praise and laud.

73

Mount Blanc the highest peak of all
In sunshine showed his face
His strength is great, his stature tall,
His title he does grace.
He stands to Father Time four square,
With Steeples famed and grand,
He proudly says, 'Climb me who dare,
and hear God's mountain band.'

Aye, Aye, Mount Blanc I'd love to climb
Thy snow-clad glacial side,
And flee from earth's low pits of crime
And there with thee abide –
Where all is pure as the white snow
That crowns thy valiant brow:
Pure crystal streams around you flow,
To slake man's thirst somehow.

Few there may be who see Mount Blanc,
And o'er the Alps do fly.
But e'en Mount Blanc can never rank
With that where Christ did die.
Then let us to Mount Calvary go,
And see Christ crucified.
Yes, plunge into the crimson flow
From our Lord's pierced side.

On and on we flew over France, the English Channel, the cliffs of Dover, and on to London. The great metropolis wasn't in a good mood that day. She seemed to be mourning for she was shrouded in a heavy dank fog that a plane dared not plunge into. After hovering above that dense fog for over an hour, the pilot received orders to go on to Hern airport, about one hundred and eight miles to the north east. It was an emergency airport which was used for such times.

In due time, we landed safely, and the Lord had preserved our "coming in" according to my Psalm. No provision had been made at Hern airport for a chap such as I was, who had been told not to walk. So I had to descend those long steps from that plane and walk across to an old fashioned bus with three high steps to ascend. Away it cantered to the airport buildings. I walked to the waiting room.

I played out and would have fallen, only an armchair was brought quickly. Faint and sick I sat down in it, and two men carried me into the room.

Shortly after entering the air terminal, someone said over the P.A. system, "Everybody will be given tickets to London by train." In a very low voice, I said to Mrs. Mainse, who was standing by my chair, "I can't go to London by train, I'll never get there." A woman who had gone to South Africa to spend a few weeks with her husband before they both returned to London, beckoned to my wife to come towards her. She said to Elva, "Did your husband say that if he had to go by train, he would never get there?" "That is what he said," Elva answered. "Well, tell him I will have a taxi here in fiteen minutes to take him right to London." At that she came walking over with my wife and said to me, "I'll have a taxi here for you in fifteen minutes to take you right to the London Airport." I replied, "God bless you. That is very kind of you." "Oh," she said, "That is only neighbourliness." I couldn't keep the tears back. Then I thought of my Psalm and praised the dear Lord again. The lady had gone back to her husband.

Again I said to Elva, "We promised to send a cable to Willa, telling her the time we would arrive in Uplands Airport in Ottawa." At that, this good Samaritan lady walked over to us again and said, "Did I hear you saying that you wanted to send a cable to Canada?" I said, "Yes, I was just saying to my wife that I promised that we would send my daughter a cable stating the time that we would arrive in Ottawa." "Well, you can't send it from here," she said, "Just write it, and I will take it to London and send it from there when we arrive." More thanks were tendered. Elva wrote the cable and she took it to London.

In a moment or two, our taxi was at the door. I was carried to it, lifted into the back seat, and cushions were placed around me. I lay on that back seat thanking the Lord for the Psalm He gave me, and the kindness of Mrs. Joyce Grenfell, a B.B.C. actress and wife of a London business man, who had truly shown God's love.

The plane from London was to take off for Canada at 4:00 p.m. and we made it into London by 3:30 p.m. I had a half an hour to be examined by the Airport Doctor and make it by wheelchair out to the plane. The doctor gave orders to the stewardess that I wasn't to walk a step, so I was carried onto the plane. At 4:00 p.m. we taxied down the runway and soon were airborne and on our way to Scotland. In two hours we landed at Prestwick and were told that there was an hour's stop. Everybody got off except my wife and I. We were allowed to stay on because of my condition. In an hour, all came back, took their seats, and the engines were started up. One engine was misfiring, so we were told that it would be another hour before flight. At the end of that hour, the fog had settled down, so the order was placed that we would have to stay all night. Everyone had left the place. The big doors were wide open, and it was very cold. I said to Mrs. Mainse, "It looks as though we will have to stay here all night." The other passengers had been taken to a hotel in Prestwick. "Oh," she said, "We can't stay here in the cold. I'll go out to see if I can find anybody." As she was walking, she met two men who were officials of some kind. She explained our plight and asked them if they could help us out. "Oh," they said, "you will have to find your pilot and steward." Crew members and even a doctor was found. The doctor asked many questions, felt my pulse, and said, "He will have to be carried off." One asked, "But where will we put them up for the night?" "I'll give them my bed," said the doctor, "and I'll find someplace else to sleep."

A wheelchair was brought onto the plane, and taking one plane seat out to get it in, they put me into the chair. A makeshift bed for Elva was put together from airplane seats, and I had a very good night's sleep in the doctor's bed. If we had flown that night, I doubt whether I would have withstood the strain of crossing the Atlantic, as it was almost too much for me, even after having a good night's rest. God bless that kind doctor.

I believe that the dear Lord knew I needed that night's rest. He caused engine trouble, then, when they got the engine fixed, He sent a dense blanket of fog. The Lord was continuing to preserve me as my Psalm said He would. Maybe someone might say, "Oh, that was just coincidence," but I believe He is "God over all, blessed forevermore." Hallelujah! You can doubt His word if you will, but I believe in His overall providences and especially so when He has given His Word to us.

The next morning, at 8:00 a.m., we took to the air again. Besides the small container of oxygen that they carried on the airplane, they took a large tank of it on board to have for me on the trip across the Atlantic. We were flying at an altitude of nineteen thousand feet, but the pressure of the air in the plane was brought down to ten thousand feet. I was very uncomfortable and had to have oxygen twenty minutes out of every hour.

Half an hour before we touched down in Iceland, we came into the clouds. Was it rough! The bouncing up and down made many sick to their stomachs, and what a relief to touch Iceland's terra firma, coming out of that bouncing region.

One hour was the time of our stop in Iceland, an island with a climite similar to British Columbia. I thought it would be an island of perpetual ice and snow.

After leaving Iceland, I became dreadfully tired and said to Elva, "I have got to get lying down someway and have a rest." Someone suggested taking out an arm rest between my seat and her seat, then I could curl up in that space. A dozen or fifteen people volunteered their small pillows so that I would be comfortable. Somebody had also turned out the lights so that it was quite dark in the plane and sleep came.

After sleeping one hour, I woke up in a cold sweat, feeling I had to get out of there; I called Elva and she awakened with a start and couldn't find the light button. Rev. Stonehouse, a travelling companion, found the light and turned it on. The stewardess rushed to give me more oxygen and my need was met.

We landed at Goose Bay, Labrador, for one hour. We then went on to Montreal, arriving at midnight. What a long day that was. It seemed as though it would never end. The pilot had radioed on ahead to the airport in Montreal to have an ambulance standing by to take us to their Red Cross Hospital room. The men came right into the plane, put me on a stretcher, carried me off, and soon I was in a comfortable bed, sleeping for nearly six hours.

At six that next morning, we were awakened by the nurse in attendance. We boarded a smaller plane for Uplands Airport in Ottawa. We didn't fly more than four to five thousand feet high, but I had to have oxygen most of the way. I was very thankful and glad that we were so near the end of our seven or eight thousand mile trip.

As we taxied into Uplands Airport, we saw quite a crowd of people to welcome us. My children standing there were a welcome sight especially. How happy we were to see them, and all who had come to welcome us home.

Three months of care and rest in the hands of the Great Physician and in my own country brought new health and strength. We were appointed again to the same two churches that we had left two years earlier, churches that were a delight to pastor. It was good medicine.

Chapter Eleven

"A Happy Heart and a Contented Mind"

I preached Sunday morning, July 4, 1953 for the first time since November 16, 1952. I'll admit I wasn't very boisterous, but I was happy to have been preserved in my going out and in my coming in, and in being in the pulpit again. For a few Sundays, I preached alternately, once a Sunday in Haley's and the next in Admaston. My good wife ably filled the pulpit once a Sunday in the other congregation. The dear people of Haley's and Admaston were so good to us, it did much to improve my health. Thanks be to God, and to my dear people of that circuit. A happy heart and a contented mind are wonderful for a person's health, and that was my portion in those churches.

During those three years of our second term on the circuit, we not only looked after the charge committed to us, but God gave me strength to build a good double garage on the parsonage, and also turn the summer kitchen into a study for the pastor. We even renovated the kitchen and dining room, building cupboards and tiling the floors.

After three more years on that circuit, we felt that we should move. In July 1956, Kingston, Ontario, became our new home. We moved on a Tuesday, and on Friday morning our Kingston area camp meetings started. As presiding Elder of the district, I had considerable responsibility thrust upon me, on top of the heavy job of moving. My son-in-law, Harold Hodgins, and my son, David, did practically all of the heavy lifting in the moving, for which I was thankful, but I marvel at the great strength of our God in sustaining my body for my tasks.

In the fall of 1957, the special session of the General Conference for Canada elected me as General Superintendent of the Eastern Canada Conference. I pleaded with them not to elect me, as my health would not stand up under the strain that would be upon one when the church was coming through the throes of church union or non-union. Nevertheless, they went ahead and elected me. I told the Conference that I would see my doctor and if he thought that I could carry on as General Superintendent, then I would. If he advised against it, they would have my resignation at once. A couple of weeks later, I told my doctor what the General Conference had done. He took another cardiograph, and then said to me, "If you just take it quietly in a church such as Kingston, you can live for a number of years, but if you continue as Superintendent, you will commit suicide." So, I asked him for a letter which he gladly gave, sent it with my resignation to the General Conference Secretary, and felt one hundred percent better. If I had never had a heart condition, it would have been a different thing entirely. I would gladly have taken the responsibility, but it was just too much. I had served for ten years as General Superintendent over the Egyptian work, and was doing that work against greater odds than Canada ever offered, but then I was hale, hearty and happy in God's work, even in the difficult duties of a Mission Field Superintendent.

The following spring of 1958, the Annual conferences, East and West voted that we take steps for church merger. I was appointed Fraternal Delegate to the Free Methodist Church Conference which met in August. A couple of days previous to our going to the Conference, we had counted the lay delegate votes for merger. I was officially delegated by the Western Canada Conference for the counting of the votes. Sixty-seven percent voted "Yes", and so it was my duty and pleasure to convey that information to the Free Methodist Conference in session.

My own congregation in Kingston was quite opposed to the merger at first but by the help of the Lord, and by careful handling, they all went along with the merger, except for one.

We were very anxious to construct a new church building in Kingston, but our congregation felt it was too heavy a responsibility. After the merging of the churches, I began advocating that we ask the Colborne Street Free Methodist Church to appoint three members to a building committee of which we would appoint three, along with Rev. B. Warren, who was pastor of Colborne Street Church, and myself. In the first meeting, I was appointed as chairman, and we began to scout around for properties. We hunted far and wide. One spot in Kingston's Polson Park area gripped us, as the property God would have us buy. I got our Kingston members of the Provincial Parliament interested in the matter. The property was bought and the sod will be broken this coming spring (1960).

During September, 1958, I assisted in the marriage of my son, David, to Norma Jean Rutledge of Galt, Ontario. David began preaching while still in his teens and I have had him speak for me several times. I'm proud to have a son following in my footsteps.

In August, 1959, I became pastor of the Wesley Chapel on Warden Avenue, Toronto. Rev. R. McCaw, whom I succeeded, had built Wesley Chapel, and to him much credit is due. It is a fine building.

In the plan of God, this was to be my last Church and, after one year, I asked to be retired. I had been forty years in the ministry. The Conference very graciously accepted my request, and granted me a retired relationship.

A Word from David Mainse

Father moved into a beautiful home at 66 Allanford Road in Agincourt, Toronto. He lived for eleven years in retirement before his death. It was a productive life. Elva is a vivacious and inspiring person, and she brightened his days with enthusiastic living. He loved the garden, the shopping trips, and the little things of life. He finished his sixty-sixth complete and studied reading of the Bible. Many poems flowed from his fertile mind and inspired heart. He was shovelling snow in that winter of his 77th year when his heart began to beat irregularly. He sat down on the steps and passed into Heaven, while held in Elva's arms.

Roy Mainse had truly "Burnt out for God," as the message from his Bible College Principal had urged him to do so long before. Parkinson's disease had plagued him in recent years, and he went through two operations, which successfully stopped the shaking of his limbs, but left him with some disability.

I tried to get to see him often, and he visited us several times. How we would worship our God together. Tears of joy would flow. The presence of God's Holy Spirit filled that house and, when walking in, I felt it was holy ground. A hearty laugh and a beautiful sense of humour are certainly necessary ingredients of a fulfilled old age, and Dad enjoyed both.

Often in times of great pressure, as a result of our international television ministry, I would find peace and tranquility in talking with Dad, and then, together, we would talk to our Father in heaven.

I would be more than delighted to hear your comments about this book. Here's my address:

100 Huntley Street
Toronto, Ontario
M4Y 2L1

or

Box 486
Niagara Falls, N.Y.
14302

The manuscript was hand-written and in its original form. I told Dad that I might publish it some day and he just laughed the laughter of a happy heart. He may have meant it just for the family, as I know that a lot of it is homey material, more of personal interest to his own loved ones. However, I pray that God will make it a great blessing to you, as He has to me.

In Christ's love & service
David Mainse

The following are some of Dad's poems written after his retirement:

Dec. 1/1960

SLEEP

When nature bows to human need,
And in its realm doth keep
Our relaxed minds in very deed, –
That process we call sleep.

How strange indeed that it should come
In twenty-four hours once:
But of all things, this is the sum –
Without it we're a dunce.

It giveth rest, makes fresh the mind,
A miracle from God:
Yet, oft we are so very blind,
And without it onward plod.

Now sleep seems next neighbour to death,
So we might fear to sleep:
For fear it might be our last breath,
Or we might dream and peep.

God doth neither slumber nor sleep,
For us His angels care:
So I shall rest in sleep as deep,
As yon bear, in its lair.

So let us sleep while God doth keep,
All those who in Him trust:
But work we must between our sleeps
Wear out instead of rust.

THE CHRISTIAN RULE

Forth-right hon'sty is the Christian rule,
'Tis double that of the business tool:
"One who would do that, would be a fool,"
So says the man from the worldly school.

Christ said, "If they make you go one mile;
Go with him twain the rest of the while:
If they ask thy coat give they cloak too."
Now that is the man who will go through.

Christ asks for only one out of ten,
Leaving us nine, because we are men.
Christ gives, and gives, and giveth again,
'Tis more than I can tell with my pen.

*Dad wrote poems such as this next one for those he
was about to join in Holy Matrimony:*

TO GILMAN AND HIS BRIDE

Our coming together is one of intent
    To honour a young man and maid,
Who've decided that life for them *could* hold
much,
    And so to this end they have prayed.

For quite a long time Gilman's tho't this thing
through,
    (And believe me, it really takes thought);
His plans are now made, and the car is all paid,
    He has reached the proud goal he has
sought.

Gilman, so kind and so helpful has been,
    A fame for himself he has won;
But a choice he must make, – a girl he must
take,
    So has finally settled for one.

85

Our hands are outstretched in blessings to him
 And the girl who stands by his side;
Our thoughts, our good wishes, our hopes for
the best
 Are extended to him and his bride.

And now,
It's just a brief matter of making the vows;
 (So little there is to be said)
The charge will be given, the ring will be set,
 A kiss, – and then they are wed.

"As you start off together in Comradeship's car,
 By the HAPPINESS CHART may you steer,
And the goal of your dreams may you proudly
attain
 And the thrill just increase with each
year."

May 10, 1962

FEELINGS VERSUS FAITH

Feelings are very funny things,
And cannot be relied upon.
They mount sometimes on eagle's wings,
And then again they're almost gone.
But faith is strong and very sure,
The evidence of things not seen,
The substance of things that endure,
Faith purges you, it makes you clean.

We oft do hear, "How do you feel"?
A rather strange and odd question:
For feelings vary a great deal,
And could be termed just a notion.
But faith takes hold of God on high,
Works wonders in the human frame,
Takes Home to heaven when you die,
And gives to you a brand new name.

Feelings are not to be despised,
Neither are they the truth, the way;
So if you'd be clever and wise,
Have faith in God. Trust God today.
Feelings are up and they are down,
But faith stands on the solid Rock;
So be a man clothed in faith's gown,
And never wear old feelings smock.

Jan. 26, 1963

THE SILLY DANCE

Together you've gathered like frogs in a pond,
To hop and to croak till tired out and wan,
Each calls to his kind in tenor and bass,
And drinks like a fish in Satan's rat race.

Frogs love the water, and sinners the dance,
They hug and they twist and take a big chance:
God ne'er intended the sexes to mate,
Until they're married by the church or state.

So youth of our day be kindly advised
And don't play the fool, but court with your
eyes:
For Satan would love to cause you to fall,
And mar your beauty and innocence all.

Will you not listen and reason a bit,
Come to your senses and possess your wit?
Don't cast yourself and your morals away,
But with all your heart cry to God and pray.

The Lord will forgive and wash your heart
white
Remove all the guilt away out of sight.
He'll give you His grace and fill you with love,
And you will be blessed from the heav'ns above.

MY CHILDREN

The Lord has given three children to me,
Merry and happy as they e'er can be:
Willa and Elaine, and David my son,
Are children, I think, as good as the run.

The whole three of them are serving the Lord,
And their lives for God are being outpoured,
Specially David, who is called of God,
To follow the path that his Dad hath trod,

A preacher I was for forty short years,
Teaching my children with joy and with tears.
Loving them into the kingdom of God
Was their dear Mother, whom they praised and
loved.

My children now have three children a piece,
To love and pray for, and watch them increase
In favour with God and their fellowmen
For soon my grandchildren will number ten.

All of their children are verily mine,
And my prayer is that, in Christ they shall
shine,
Doing the Lord's will with a cheerful heart,
And walk in the light of God's divine chart.

GOD'S WORD

An anvil is God's holy Word:
It stands complete – Thus saith the Lord.
"Hammer away, ye hostile hands:
Your hammers break, God's anvil stands."

This anvil firm, it will remain:
It will not break, fore'er 'twill reign,
The devil may cast forth his spume
To tarnish it. 'Tis not its doom.

The Word of God indeed will stand,
While hammers break like ropes of sand –
Men try their luck with doctrines false
To propogate their evil cults.

But both of these will failures prove,
For by God's Word they shall remove,
So hammer on deceitful hands:
"Your hammers break, God's anvil stands".

WHY WORRY!

Why worry you? Such is not trust.
Worry eats as corroding rust:
It breaks the heart, it spoils the life,
Trouble there is 'tween trust and strife.

Help is in God, cast all your care
On Him Who will your burdens bear:
His promise is, He'll comfort give,
And only then you'll start to live.

Trust thou in God, your mighty Aid,
As you thro' troubles seem to wade;
O falter not, O do not fail,
Because your hands are weak and frail.

There's One above, Who giveth grace,
That calms the heart, that shines the face:
His promise is ye shall receive,
Grace for each day if you'll believe.

Have faith in God, give worry wings
To fly away as your heart sings –
A paean of praise for all Gods ways,
And for His help thro' future days.

March 3, 1965

ROBIN RED BREAST

As Spring is on the march again,
Rollicking robin, our very dear friend
Has March the third been seen and heard –
O, what a brave and courageous bird.

He sings on the maple's topmost branch,
And chirups his way to the cattle ranch:
The snows of Spring he does defy,
So it just has to say good-bye.

He builds his nest in the apple tree,
Where the dear children can't help but see
The sky blue eggs in number four,
Which in two weeks will be no more.

But four little mouths will open wide,
And down their throats slippery worms will
slide,
Until the nest becomes too small
For speckled red breasts who know it all.

Out on the air they flutter and fly,
While Mother Robin does plaintively cry,
"Just over there is a big tom-cat,
Who would eat a bird like a measley rat."

FATHER TIME

Time was, and is, and e'en shall be,
As long as God in heav'n may see,
That it is good for mortal man
To do His will, fulfill His plan.

But Father Time is growing old.
His hands are weak, his feet are cold,
His heart contracts, then groweth strong,
Beating away with rhythmic song.

Twelve hours of day, twelve hours of night,
Is the average of dark and light:
Though he sleeps not, yet we may sleep,
In peace and quiet, profound and deep.

For thousands of years time's on the go,
Sometimes it's fast, sometimes it's slow
But steadily it ploddeth on
Whether it's flush or weak and wan.

He waiteth not for anyone,
Even the stars join in and run
Their daily course at his command
In the hour glass of running sand.

The sun is Time's great meas'ring stick,
It burns slowly Time's ending wick:
When it's finished, Time's no more
Eternity then opens the door.

FAME

Fame – it is a deceptive thing,
Yet it does try to bravely sing,
Of all the things that it has done,
And make out 'tis a lot of fun.

Fame – it is a glamorous thing,
Making some bells so loudly ring,
Until vain man sits up and stares,
And with its vanity he shares.

Fame – it is a subversive thing.
To a man's heart it e'er will cling,
Until it chokes the soul within,
And leaves the mark of damning sin.

Fame – it is a delusive thing,
Always fluttering on the wing,
Settling rarely here or there;
So that vain man cannot it share.

So why be fooled by fame's brash show,
All is not gold that tries to glow,
Fame is a thing that lures and damns,
And leaves behind most fearful qualms.

Feb. 16, 1966

BIG THINGS

Think big, pray big and believe big,
Don't stop at a wee scrawny fig –
For God's great and omnipotent,
Able to do the magnificient.

Our God is big, big things He'll do,
And He'll see you all the way thro' –
Yes thro' the mire and thro' the clay,
Giving vict'ry all of the way.

Act big and hon'r the God you serve,
He'll give fibre and lots of nerve –
To see you thro' the trying times,
And give dollars instead of dimes.

So honour Him by a faith big,
by actions more than nod of wig –
For God is great in faithfulness,
And He's ready to love and bless.

THE SAINTS' ENTRANCE INTO HEAVEN

O, what is that my friend I see
Across that great expanse?
O, that you see is the Life-tree,
That we may eat perchance.

By faith we knock on Heaven's gate
To seek admission there;
And we are told, Ye are not late
As ye are men of prayer.

The gate swings wide, "Come in," is cried,
"Ye saints of God, Most High;
And ye shall ever more abide,
Where none e'er say, 'good-bye'."

In, in, we go upon tip-toe
To see the glory land
Our spirits slow begin to glow
For isn't heaven grand.

We've joined the throng of the redeemed
Around the glassy sea,
Where all of heaven's much esteemed
Feast on the sweet Life-tree.

Up here we sing, God's praises ring,
And "Holy, Holy," cry;
The angel's 'round God's throne do wing,
And we with joy draw nigh.

"Well done, well done," the Lord cries out,
"Let harp and fiddle strum!
The saints join in, cry out and shout,
"Behold thy kingdom's come."

DAVID

For thee we prayed in faith and love,
To the great God, who is above.
For give long years we hoped and prayed,
Wondering why God's hand was staid.

It seemed preposterous to us,
That we be denied a boy thus:
But at long last a son was born
August, the thirteenth, in the morn.

At age of twelve his mother died,
And from his heart he weeping cried –
"I will meet you in heav'n, I will,
I will." That's his aim even still.

In a few years he heard God's call,
And thank the Lord he didn't stall,
At the hindrances in the way,
But o'ercame them by night and day.

A good preacher he has become,
Preaching the Word that does ransom,
Man from his lost and ruined estate,
And from death that would be his fate.

Life eternal is his great theme,
To all of mankind it would seem,
A reality and next a dream,
The best of life, even its cream.

David, my son, proclaim God's Word,
For many men have never heard,
The message which God has giv'n you,
And to that Word be ever true.

O'er yonder we will meet again,
When through with life, paper and pen,
We'll hear God say, "Well done, well done,
The race you have successfully run".

From the flyleaf of Dad's Bible:

My Desire

I want to be a man of God,
A man of true and gracious worth:
Preaching the Word with love on fire,
That men may find the second birth.

I want to be a worker true,
A worker ne'er to be ashamed:
Lifting burdens from weary hearts
Of sinful men who've been new named.

I want to see God's will well done,
Both here and in the hereafter,
Just as the hosts of heaven do
In all the Book and each chapter.

22/5/58.
R.L. Mainse

From the Year Book of Annesley College, 1948:

Our heart's desire is so to impress for good the lives of all with whom we come in touch, that they will be better on account of our having made contact with them.

We wish to show how we may gain the secret of right contact, then, how to make our contact effectual, and conclude with the rewards of loving service rendered.

In the first place, things that count for success seem just beyond our reach. We try to influence people for good, but our best efforts of themselves prove futile; and worse than useless, even harmful. The secret of successful contact is found in the magnetic Son of God, who never made a failure in any of His many human relationships.

Ere we can expect success with our fellow men, we must contact Christ; and receive of His fullness, which imparts to us life, movement, and real worthwhile being. We, through that supernatural Presence, are able to give the living, drawing touch to our otherwise impotent, fireless contact. Our part is to keep the vital contact with Jesus, and lift Him up. He, unseen to the natural eye, will do the impossible through us; and we shall have the joy of seeing the divine-human touch connecting the object of our contact to the Source of all magnetic power.

Lastly, we shall be rewarded for our God-blessed contacts, as though they were solely wrought by us; when, in reality, all the credit belongs to Him, whom we lifted up from the earth, thus making contact possible. It is true, we think sometimes of the rewards that God has promised to His faithful servant. How wonderful they are! They are truly too great for us to receive, but not too great for God to give. On these conditions we all should seek to contact our fellow men, and be a blessing to our day and generation.

R.L. Mainse,
Principal of Annesley.